A Childhood
in
Brittany,
Eighty Years Ago

By

Anne Douglas Sedgwick
(Mrs. Basil de Sélincourt)
- 1873-1935 -

Merchant Books
1919

"Keransiflan and I, sitting on our wheelbarrow, were allowed to go on eating in peace"

"Keransiflan and I, sitting on our wheelbarrow, were allowed to go on eating in peace."

A Childhood
in
Brittany,
Eighty Years Ago

Anne Douglas Sedgwick

With illustrations by Paul de Leslie

Merchant Books

Contents

This little sheaf of childish memories has been put together from many talks, in her own tongue, with an old French friend. The names of her relatives have, by her wish, been changed to other names, taken from their Breton properties, or slightly altered, while preserving the character of the Breton original.

Cover: Quimper

CHAPTER I

Quimper & Bonne Maman

I WAS born at Quimper in Brittany on the first of August, 1833, at four o'clock in the morning, and I have been told that I looked about me resolutely and fixed a steady gaze on the people in the room, so that the doctor said, "She is not blind, at all events."

The first thing I remember is a hideous doll to which I was passionately attached. It belonged to the child of one of the servants, and my mother, since I would not be parted from it, gave this child, to replace it, a handsome doll. It had legs stuffed with sawdust and a clumsily painted cardboard head, and on this head it wore a *bourrelet*. The *bourrelet* was a balloon-shaped cap made of plaited wicker, and was worn by young children to protect their heads when they fell. We, too, wore them in our infancy, and I remember that I was very proud when wearing mine and that I thought it a very pretty head-dress.

I could not have been more than three years old when I was brought down to the *grand salon* to be shown to a friend of my father's, an Englishman, on his way to England from India, and a pink silk dress I then wore, and my intense satisfaction in it, is my next memory. It had a stiff little bodice and skirt, and there were pink rosettes over my ears. But I could not have been a pretty child, for my golden hair, which grew abundantly in later years, was then very scanty, and my mouth was large. I was stood upon a mahogany table, of which I still see the vast and polished spaces beneath me, and Mr. John Dobray, when I was introduced to him by my proud father, said, "So this is Sophie."

Mr. Dobray wore knee-breeches, silk stockings, and a high stock. I see my father, too, very tall, robust, and fair, with the pleasantest face. But my father's figure fills all my childhood. I was his pet and darling. When I cried and was naughty, my mother would say: "Take your daughter. She tires me and is insufferable." Then my father would take me in his arms and walk up and down with me while he sang me to sleep with old Breton songs. One of these ran:

> Jésus péguen brasvé,
> Plégar douras néné;
> Jésus péguen brasvé,
> Ad ondar garan té!

This, as far as I remember, means, "May Jesus be happy, and may His grace make us all happy."

At other times my father played strange, melancholy old Breton tunes to me on a violin, which he held upright on his knee, using the bow across it as though it were a 'cello. He was, though untaught, exceedingly musical, and played by ear on the clavecin[1] anything he had heard. It must have been from him that I inherited my love of music, and I do not remember the time that I was not singing.

I see myself, also, at the earliest age, held before my father on his saddle as we rode through woods. He wore an easy Byronic collar and always went bareheaded. He spent most of his time on horseback, visiting his farms or hunting.

My father was of a wealthy bourgeois family of Landerneau,[2] and it must have been his happy character and love of sport rather than his wealth–he was Master of Hounds and always kept the pack–that made him popular in Quimper, for the gulf between the *bourgeoisie* and the *noblesse* was almost impassable. Yet not only was he popular, but he had married my mother, who was of an ancient Breton family, the Rosvals. One of the Rosvals fought in the Combats de Trente[3] against the English, and the dying and thirsty Beaumanoir to whom it was said on

---

[1] Harpsichord; carillon keyboard
[2] A commune in Finistère department in Bretagne in northwestern France
[3] The Combat of the Thirty (26 March 1351)

that historic day, "Bois ton sang, Beaumanoir," was a cousin of theirs.

My mother was a beautiful woman with black hair and eyes of an intense dark blue. She was unaware of her own loveliness, and was much amused one day when her little boy, after gazing intently at her, said, "*Maman*, you are very beautiful." She repeated this remark, laughing, to my father, on which he said, "Yes, my dear, you are."

My mother was extremely proud, and not at all flattered that she should be plain Mme. Kerouguet, although she was devoted to my father and it was the happiest *ménage*[4]. I remember one day seeing her bring to my father, looking, for all her feigned brightness, a little conscious, some new visiting-cards she had had printed, with the name of Kerouguet reduced to a simple initial, and followed by several of the noble ancestral names of her own family.

"What's this?" said my father, laughing.

"We needed some new cards," said my mother, "and I dislike so much the name of Kerouguet."

But my father, laughing more than ever, said:

"Kerouguet you married and Kerouguet you must remain," and the new cards had to be relinquished.

My mother, with her black hair and blue eyes, had a charming nose of the sort called "*un nez Roxalane*."[5] It began very straight and fine, but had a flattened little plateau on the tip which we called "*la promenade de maman*." My memory of her then is of a very active, gay, authoritative young woman, going to balls, paying and receiving visits, and riding out with my father, wearing the sweeping habit of those days and an immense beaver hat and plume.

---

[4] Household
[5] Her nose was of the curious, witty variety, just escaping impertinence, what the French called 'un nez a la Roxelane' *from* 'Portraits & Backgrounds' By Evangeline Wilbour Blashfield

"Quimper is an old town"

"Quimper is an old town"

Quimper is an old town, and the *hôtels* of the *noblesse*, all situated in the same quarter and on a steep street, were of blackened, crumbling stone. From *porte-cochères*[6] one entered the courtyards, and the gardens behind stretched far into the country.

In the courtyard of our *hôtel* was a stone staircase, with elaborate carvings, like those of the Breton churches, leading to the upper stories, but for use there were inner staircases. My mother's boudoir, the *petit salon*, the *grand salon*, the *salle-à-manger*, and the billiard-room were on the ground floor and gave out upon the garden.

The high walls that ran along the street and surrounded the garden were concealed by plantations of trees, so that one seemed to look out into the country. Flower beds were under the salon-windows, and there were long borders of wild strawberries that had been transplanted from the woods, as my

---

[6] Literally "coach gate," also called a carriage porch

mother was very fond of them. Fruit-trees grew against the walls, and beyond the groves and flower beds and winding gravel paths was an orchard, with apricot-, pear-, and apple-trees, and the clear little river Odel, with its washing-stones, where the laundry-maids beat the household linen in the cold, running water.

It was pleasant to hear the *clap-clap-clap* on a hot summer day. Is it known that the pretty pied water-wagtail is called *la lavandière* from its love of water and its manner of beating up and down its tail as our washerwomen wield their wooden beaters?

Beyond the river were the woods where I often rode with my father, and beyond the woods distant ranges of mountains. I looked out at all this from my nursery-windows, with their frame of climbing-roses and heliotrope. Near my window was a great lime-tree of the variety known as American. The vanilla-like scent of its flowers was almost overpowering, and all this fragrance gave my mother a headache, and she had to have her room moved away from the garden to another part of the house. How clearly I see this room of my mother's, with its high, canopied four-poster bed and the pale-gray paper on the walls covered with yellow fleurs-de-lis!

The wall-paper in my father's room was one of the prettiest I have ever seen, black, all bespangled with bright butterflies. Of the *grand salon* I remember most clearly the high marble mantelpiece, upheld by hounds sitting on their haunches. On this mantelpiece was a huge *boule*[7] clock, two tall candelabra of Venetian glass, and two figures in *vieux Saxe* of a marquis and a marquise that filled us with delight. On each side of the fireplace were two Louis XV court chairs—chairs, that is, with only one arm, to admit of the display of the great hoop-skirts of the period. I remember, too, our special delight in the foot-stools, which were of mahogany, shaped rather like gondolas and cushioned in velvet; for we could sit inside them and make them rock up and down.

The houses of the *noblesse* swarmed with servants; many of them were married, and their children, and even their grandchildren, lived on with our family in patriarchal fashion.

---

[7] Globe

Men and maids all wore the costumes of their respective Breton cantons, exceedingly beautiful some of them, stiff with heavy embroideries, the strange caps of the women fluted and ruffled, adorned with lace, rising high above their heads and falling in long lappets upon their shoulders, or perched on their heads like butterflies. These caps were decorated with large gold pins and dangling golden pendants, and these and the materials for the costumes were handed down in the peasants' families from generation to generation. My young nurse Jeannie—there was an old nurse called Gertrude—wore a skirt of bright-blue woolen stuff and a black-cloth bodice opening in a square over a net fichu thickly embroidered with *paillettes* of every color. Hers was the small flat cap of Quimper, with the odd foolscap excrescence, rather like the horn of a rhinoceros, curving forward over the forehead. Needless to say, the servants did not do their daily work in this fine array; while that went on they were enveloped from head to foot in large aprons.

The servants and the peasants in the Brittany of those days had a pretty custom of always using the *thou* when addressing their masters or the Deity, thus inverting the usual association of this mode of address; for to each other they said *you*, and on their lips this was the familiar word, and the *thou* implied respect. Our servants were of the peasant class, but service altered and civilized them very much, and while no peasant spoke anything but Breton, they talked in an oddly accented French. I remember a pretty example of this in a dear old man who served my little cousin Guénolé du Jacquelot du Bois-Laurel. Guénolé and I, because of some naughtiness, were deprived of strawberries one day at our supper, and the fond old man, grieving over the discomfiture of his little master, said, or, rather chanted, half in condolence, and half in playful consolation: "Oh, le pauvre Guénolé, que tu es désolé !" accenting the *o* in a very droll fashion.

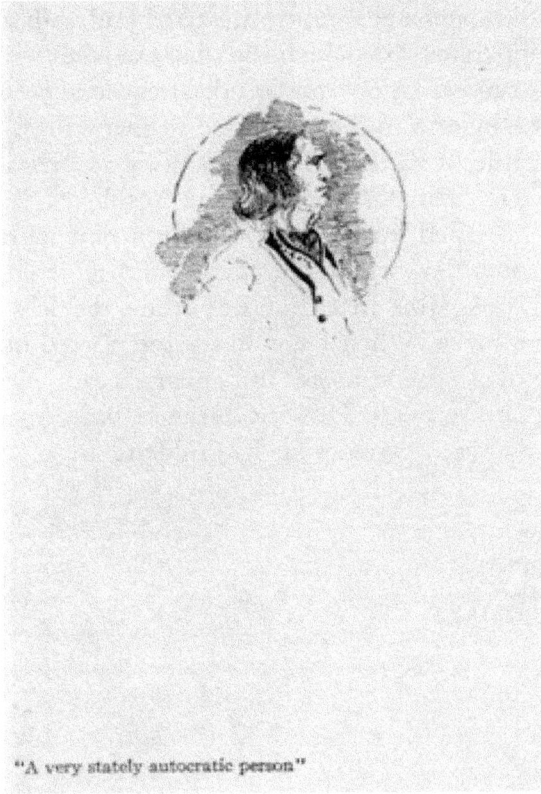

"A very stately autocratic person"

"A very stately autocratic person"

The servants were all under the orders of a very stately autocratic person, the steward or major-domo. It was he who directed the service from behind his master's chair at the head of the table and he who prescribed the correct costume for the servants. His wife had charge of Jeannie and of me; it was she who, when two little sisters and a brother had been added to the family, took us down to our breakfast and supervised the meal. We had it in a little tower-room on the ground floor, milk soup or gruel and the delicious bread and butter of Brittany.

We lunched and dined at ten and five—such were the hours of those days—with our parents in the dining-room, and it was here that one of the most magnificent figures of my childhood appears; for my devoted father brought me back from Paris one day a splendid mechanical pony, life-sized and with a real pony-skin, the apparatus by which he was moved simulating an exhilarating canter. Upon this steed, after dessert, we children mounted one by one, and we resorted to many ruses in order to get the first ride of the day. This dear pony accompanied all my childhood. He lost his hair as the result of an unhappy experiment we tried upon him, scrubbing him with hot water and soap, one day when we were unobserved. He had a melancholy look after that, but was none the less active and none the less loved. When I saw his dismembered body lying in the garret of a grand-niece not many years ago I felt a contraction of the heart. How he brought back my youth, and since that how many generations had ridden him!

We played in the garden at Quimper

"We played in the garden at Quimper"

We played at being horses, too, driving each other in the garden, where we spent most of our days when at Quimper. Strange to say, even while we were thus occupied, we always wore veils tightly tied over our bonnets and faces to preserve our skins from the sun. We all wore, even in earliest childhood, stiff little dresses with closely fitting boned bodices. My sister Eliane was delicate and wore flannel next her skin; but my only underclothing consisted of cambric chemise, petticoats, and drawers, these last reaching to my ankles and terminating in frills that fell over the foot in its little sandaled shoe. When I came back from a wonderful stay, later on, of four or five years in England, a visit that revolutionized my ideas of life, I wore the easy dress of English children, and had bare arms, much to my mother's dismay. Another change that England wrought in me was that I was filled with discomfort when I saw the peasants kneeling before us at Loch-ar-Brugg, our country home; for in those days, although the Revolution had passed over France, it was still the custom for peasants to kneel before their masters, and my mother felt it right and proper that they should do so. I begged her not to allow it, but she insisted upon the ceremony to her dying day, and only when I came as mistress to Loch-ar-Brugg with my children and grandchildren was it discontinued.

Another early memory is the long row of family portraits in the *salle-à-manger*. I think I must have looked up at these from my father's shoulder as he walked up and down with me, singing to me while my mother went on with her interrupted dessert, for the awe that some of them inspired in me seems to stretch back to babyhood. Some were so dark and severe that it was natural they should frighten a baby; but it was a pastel, in flat, pale tones, of an old lady with high powdered hair, whose steady, forbidding gaze followed me up and down the room, that frightened me most This was an elder sister of my grandmother's, a March'-Inder, who, dressed as a man, had fought with her husband and daughter in the war of the Chouans[8] against the republic. Her husband was killed, and her daughter, taken prisoner by a French officer, had hanged herself, so the family story ran, to escape insult. Another portrait of a great-grandmother enchanted me then, as it has done ever since, a charming young woman seated, with her hands folded before her, her golden hair unpowdered, her dress of citron-colored satin brocaded with bunches of pale, bright flowers. And there was a portrait of my grandmother in youth, with black hair and eyes as black as jet. I thought her very

---

[8] The "Chouans" were the French royalists of Maine and Brittany who revolted against the French conventions in 1792

ugly, and could never associate her with my dearly loved *bonne maman.*

I must delay no longer in introducing this most important member of the family, my mother's mother, with whom we lived, for the old Quimper *hôtel* was her dower-house.

Poor *bonne maman!* I see her still, in her deep arm-chair, always dressed in a long gown of puce-colored satin, a white lace mantilla, caught up with a small bunch of artificial buttercups, on her white hair. She wore white-thread lace mittens that reached to her elbows, and her thin, white hands were covered with old-fashioned rings. My mother was her favorite daughter, and I, as the eldest child of this favorite, was specially cherished. Both of *bonne maman's* parents had been guillotined in the Revolution. I do not think her husband was of much comfort to her. He came to Quimper only for short stays. He was *directeur des Ponts et chausées*[9] for the district, but also a deputy in Paris, and these political duties, according to him, gave him no leisure for family life. He was at least ten years younger than *bonne maman,* very gay and witty, *l'homme du monde*[10] in all the acceptations of the term, full of deference to *bonne maman,* whom he treated like a queen, with respectful salutes and gallant kissings of the hand. He seemed very fond of his home at Quimper when he was in it, but he seldom graced it with his presence.

When I went up to see *bonne maman* in the morning, she would give me her thumb to kiss, an odd formality, since she was full of demonstrations of affection toward me. I did not find the salute altogether agreeable, since *bonne maman* took snuff constantly, and her delicate thumb and forefinger were strongly impregnated with the smell of tobacco. Taking me on her knees, she would then very gravely ask to see my little finger, and when I held it up, she would scrutinize it carefully, and from its appearance tell me whether I had been good or naughty. Beside her chair *bonne maman* had always a little table, the round polished top surrounded by a low brass railing. On this were ranged a number of toilet implements, her glasses, scent-bottle,

---

[9] Manager of bridges and roads
[10] Man of the world

work-bag, and various knickknacks. A very unique implement, I imagine, was a little stick of polished wood, with a tuft of cotton wool tied by a ribbon at one end. This she used, when her maid had powdered her hair or face, to dust off the superfluous powder, and I can see her now, her little mirror in one hand, the ribboned stick in the other, turning her head from side to side and softly brushing the tuft over her brow and chin. The table was always carried down with her to the *petit salon*, where, her morning toilet over, she was borne in her chair by means of the handles that projected before and behind it.

Bonne maman had an old carriage, an old horse, and an old coachman. None of these was ever used, since she never went out except on Easter day, when she was carried in a sedan-chair to hear mass at the cathedral nearby. The sedan-chair was gray-green with bunches of flowers painted on it, and upholstered with copper-colored satin. It was carried by four bearers in full Breton costume. They wore jackets of a bright light blue, beautifully embroidered along the edges with disks of red, gold, and black; red sashes, tied round their waists, hung to the knees; their full kneebreeches were white, their shoes black, and their stockings of white wool. Like all the peasants of that time, they wore their hair long, hanging over their shoulders, and their large, round Breton hats were of black felt tied with a thick chenille cord of red, blue, and black, which was held to the brim at one side by a golden fleur-de-lis and that, had a scapular dangling from the end. Within the chair sat my grandmother, dressed, as always, in puce color; but this gala costume was of brocade, flowers of a paler shade woven upon a dark ground, and the lace mantilla of every-day wear was replaced by a sort of white tulle head-dress, gathered high upon her head and falling over her breast and shoulders. I remember her demeanor in church on these great occasions, her gentle authority and *recueillement*,[11] and the glance of grave reproach for my mother, who was occupied in looking about her and in making humorous comments on the odd clothes and attitude of her fellow-

---

[11] Reverence

worshipers. On all other days the curé[12] brought the communion to my grandmother in her room. I remember the first of these communions that I witnessed. I was sitting on *bonne maman's* bed when the curé entered, accompanied by his acolytes in red and white, and I was highly interested when I recognized in one of these important personages the cook's little boy. The curé was going to lift me from the bed, but *bonne maman* said: "No; let her stay. When you are gone I will explain to her the meaning of what she sees." This she attempted to do, but not, I imagine, with much success. Old Gertrude, Jeannie's chief in the nursery, had of course already told me of *le petit Jesus*, and I had learned to repeat, "Seigneur, je vous donne coeur." But *bonne maman* was grieved to find that I did not yet know "Our Father."

"Sophie does not know her Pater," she said to my mother. "She must learn it."

"Oh, she is too young to learn it," said my mother. But *bonne maman* was not at all satisfied with this evasion and saw that the prayer was taught to me. She was very devout and confessed twice a week; but more than this, she was the best of women. I never heard her speak ill of any one or saw her angry at any time, nor did I ever see her give way to mirth, though I remember a species of silent laughter that at times shook her thin body.

---

[12] Parish priest

"*Bonne maman* was devoted
to my father"

"Bonne maman was devoted to my father"

Bonne maman was devoted to my father, even more devoted than to her own sons, of whom she had had eight. They had been so severely brought up by her, but especially, I feel sure, by my grandfather, that through exaggerated respect and absurd ceremony they almost trembled during the short audiences granted to them by their parents. My father trembled before nobody. He was always cheerful, good-tempered, and kind. During our life at Quimper he was not much at home, as he had a horror of receptions and visits,—all the bother, as he said, of social life,—and the time not spent in hunting was fully occupied in seeing after his farms, his crops, and his peasants. Therefore, when he came back for a three-or-four-days' stay with us, it was a delight to young and old. I see him now, sitting in a low chair beside *bonne maman's* deep *bergère*, his head close to hers, his pipe between his teeth,—yes, his pipe—for *bonne maman* not only permitted, but even commanded, him to smoke in her presence, so much did she value every moment of the time he could be with her. So they smiled at each other while they talked,—the snowy, powdered old head and the fair young one enveloped in the midst of smoke,—understanding each other perfectly; and although their opinions were diametrically opposed, politics was their favorite theme. They must have taught me their respective battle-cries, for I well remember that, riding my father's knee and listening, while he varied the gait from trot to gallop, I knew just when to cry out, "*Vive le Roi!*"[13] in order to please *bonne maman*, and "*Vive la République!* " to make papa laugh. When disputes occurred in *bonne maman's* room, they were between my father and mother, if that can be called a dispute where one is so gay and so imperturbable. It was *maman* who brought all the heat and vehemence to these differences, and, strange to say, *bonne maman* always took my father's side against her beloved daughter. My mother's quick temper, I may add, displayed itself toward me pretty frequently in slaps and whippings, no doubt well deserved, for I was a naughty, willful child; whereas in all my life I never received a punishment from my father. I remember his distress on one of these occasions and how he said, "It is unworthy to beat someone who cannot retaliate." To which my mother, flushed and indignant, replied, "It would indeed need only that." She was a charming and lovable woman, but I loved my father best.

---

[13] Long live the King!

"I heard music constantly"

"I heard music constantly"

Bonne maman was very musical, and in the *petit salon*, when she was installed there for the day, I heard music constantly, performed by two young *protégés* of the house. One of these was Mlle. Ghislaine du Guesclin, the youngest descendant of our great Breton hero. It was a very poor, very haughty family, and extremely proud of its origin. Ghislaine's father, the Marquis du Guesclin (for with a foolish conceit he had separated the particle from the name) had died, leaving his daughter penniless and recommending her to my grandfather, who placed her as *dame de compagnie* beside my mother and *bonne maman*. Ghislaine was an excellent musician, and their relation was of the happiest. The other *protégé* was called Yves le Grand, and was the son of *bonne maman's coiffeur.* His story was curious. As a boy of fourteen or fifteen he had come three times a week to wash the windows and doors, and while he worked he sang all sorts of Breton songs and strange airs that, as was learned later, were his own improvisations. *Bonne maman,* noticing his talent, had him taken to Paris by her husband, and he was educated in the conservatory, where, after ten years of admirable study, he took the second prize. He returned to Quimper, and earned a handsome livelihood by giving pianoforte lessons while remaining in a sense our private musician, for he was much attached to us all and accompanied us on all our travels. Ghislaine sang in a ravishing fashion, and Yves accompanied her on the clavecin that stood in the *petit salon,* mingling the grave accents of his baritone with her clear soprano. When I first heard them I was almost stupefied by the experience, cuddling down into *bonne maman's* arms, my head sunk between her cheek and shoulder, but listening with such absorption and with such evident appreciation that *bonne maman* loved me more than ever for the community of taste thus revealed between us.

I must often have tired her. I was a noisy, active child, and sometimes when I sat on her knee and prattled incessantly in my shrill, childish voice, she would pass her hand over her forehead and say: "Not so loud, darling; not so loud. You pierce my ear-drums; and you know that *le bon Dieu* has said that one must never speak without first turning one's tongue seven times round in one's mouth." At this I would gaze wide-eyed at *bonne maman* and try involuntarily to turn my tongue seven times, an exercise at which I have never been successful. I may add in parenthesis that I have often regretted it. Another amusing adage I heard at the same time from Gertrude. If a child made a face, it was told to take care lest the wind should turn, and the face remain like that forever. I was much troubled by this idea on one occasion when maman and Ghislaine had been to a fancy dress ball. Ghislaine told me next day about the dances and dresses. *Maman* had danced a minuet dressed in a Pompadour costume, and she herself had gone as a deviless, with a scarlet-and-black dress and little golden horns in her black hair. I felt this to have been a very dangerous proceeding, for if *le bon Dieu* had noticed

Ghislaine's travesty, He might have made the wind turn, and she would then have remained a deviless and been forced to live in hell for all eternity.

A pretty custom at that time and in that place was that the young matrons who went to such balls and dinner-parties were expected to bring little silk bags in which they carried home to their children the left-over sweetmeats of the dessert; so that we children enjoyed these entertainments as much as Ghislaine and *maman.*

"Ghislaine taught me my letters"

"Ghislaine taught me my letters"

Ghislaine taught me my letters from a colored alphabet in the *petit salon,* showing an angelic patience despite my yawns and whimperings. My memories of the alphabet are drolly intermingled with various objects in the *petit salon* that from the earliest age charmed my attention. One of these was an immense tortoise-shell mounted on a tripod, and another a vast Chinese umbrella of pale yellow satin, with silk and crystal fringes, that, suspended from the ceiling in front of the long windows that gave on the garden, was filled with flowers. This had been an ingenious contrivance of my father's, and *bonne maman* found it as bewitching as I did, never failing to say to visitors, after the first greetings had passed: "Do you see my Chinese umbrella?" When I had learned seven letters *bonne maman* gave me four red *dragées de baptême*,—the sugar-almonds that are scattered at christenings,—and promised me as many more for each new attainment. Thus sustained, I was able to master the alphabet and to pass by slow degrees to Æsop's Fables, with pictures and a yellow cover. It was later on that Ghislaine began to coach me in all the *départements* of France and their capitals. *Maman* lent a hand in this and instituted a method that was singularly successful. I still laugh in remembering how at any time of the day, before guests, at meals, or while we were at play, she might suddenly call out to us, "Gers!" for instance, to which one must instantly reply "Auch." Or else it was "Gironde!" and the reply, "Bordeaux," must follow without hesitation. If I replied correctly, I was given fifty centimes; if incorrectly, I received a slap. I used to dream of the *départements* and their capitals at night. One rainy day I was playing in the *petit salon*, lying at full length on the floor and making a castle of blocks, when *maman*, coming suddenly out of the library, a great tray of books in her arms, cried out to me as she came, walking very quickly, "Gare!"[14] Without moving and without looking up, I replied obediently, "Nîmes" (the capital of Gard), and an avalanche of books descended upon me, poor *maman* and her tray coming down with a dreadful clatter. *Maman* was not hurt, but very much afraid that I was.

When she found us both, except for a few bruises, safe and sound, she went off into a peal of laughter, and I followed suit,

---

14 "Watch out!"

much relieved; for I had imagined for one moment that I had made a mistake in my answer, and I found the punishment too severe.

"You are sure I have not hurt you, darling?" said *maman*, kissing me; and I replied with truth:

"No, *Maman*; but I should have preferred the *gifle*."[15] On that day, instead of fifty centimes, I received a franc for consolation.

It was not until my brother's tutor came to us, when I was eight or nine years old, that I ever had any teacher but Ghislaine.

Poor Ghislaine! Hers was a rather sad story. She had great beauty, thick, black hair, white skin, her small prominent nose full of distinction, but one strange peculiarity: there were no nails on her long, pointed fingers. This, while not ugly, startled one in noticing her hands. As I have said, she had been left penniless, and it was difficult in France, then as now, to find a husband for a *jeune fille sans dot*.[16] Ghislaine only begged that he should be a gentleman. But after *bonne maman's* death, when we had gone to live in Paris, Ghislaine was left behind with my aunt's family, and they finally arranged a marriage for her with a notary. My mother was much distressed by this prosaic match. She had for a time cherished the romantic project of a marriage between Ghislaine and Yves, who, besides being an artist, was the best of men, sincere, devoted, and delicate.

For a descendant of du Guesclin the *coiffeur's* son would, however, have been as inappropriate as was the notary. The latter, too, was an excellent man, and Ghislaine was not unhappy with him.

---

[15] A slap
[16] Girl without a dowry

CHAPTER II

Eliane

AN important event in my child life was the birth of my sister Eliane. I remember coming in from the garden one day with a little basket full of cockchafers that I had found, and running to show them to *maman*. She was lying in her large bed, with its four carved bedposts and high canopy, and, smiling faintly, she said: "Oh, no, my little girl; take them away. They will creep and fly over everything." I was, however, so much disappointed at this reception of my gift that *maman*, bending from her pillows, selected an especially beautiful green cockchafer[17] and said that that one, at all events, she would keep. When next morning I was told that I had a little sister, old Gertrude, in answer to my eager, astonished questions, informed me that it was the cockchafer who, fed on milk, had become very large during the night and had given birth to a baby cockchafer, which it had presented to my mother. This story of the cockchafer became a family jest, and later on, after my mother had had four children, I remembered that when cockchafers were referred to she would laugh and say: "No! no! No more cockchafers for me, if you please! I have had enough of their gifts."

The story, which was repeated to me on the occasion of each subsequent birth, made a rather painful impression upon me. I did not like the idea of the baby cockchafer. Nor did I like my little sister Eliane into whom the cockchafer had grown. *Maman* remained in bed for a long time and paid no more attention to me, and I was deeply jealous. I was no longer allowed to go in

---

[17] Any of various European beetles

and out of her room as had been my wont, and when my father took me in his arms and carried me gently in to see my little sister, and bent with me over the small pink cradle so that I might give her a kiss, I felt instead a violent wish to bite her. One day I was authorized to rock Eliane while my father and mother talked together. I was much pleased by this mark of confidence, and I slipped into the cradle, unnoticed, my horrible doll Josephine, all untidy and disheveled, not to say dirty, so that she, too, might have a rocking. She lay cheek to cheek with Eliane, already a young lady ten days old, and the contact of this cold, clammy cheek woke my little sister, who began to cry so loudly that, in order to quiet her, I rocked with might and main, and unless papa had rushed to the rescue it is probable that Eliane and Josephine would have been tossed out upon the floor. Jeannie was at once summoned to take me away in disgrace, and in *bonne maman's* room I was consoled by two *dragées*, one white, I remember, and one pink.

"You love your little sister, don't you, my darling?" asked *bonne maman*, to whom Jeannie related the affair of the rocking.

"No," I replied, the pink *dragée* in my mouth.

"Why not, dear?"

"She is horrid," I said. And as *bonne maman*, much distressed, continued to question and expostulate, I burst, despite the dragées, into a torrent of tears and cried: "She is bad! She is ugly! She cries!"

Eliane's christening was a grand affair. Her godmother was *bonne maman*, and her godfather my uncle de Salabéry, who brought her a casket in which was a cup and saucer in enamel and also an enamel egg-cup and tiny, round egg-spoon, and this I thought very silly, since Eliane, like the cockchafer, ate only milk. The casket was of pale-blue velvet, and had Eliane's name written upon it in golden letters. She was carried to the cathedral by her nurse, who wore a gray silk dress woven with silver fleurs-de-lis, a special silk, with its silver threads, made in Brittany. The bodice opened on a net guimpe[18] thickly embroidered with white beads. The apron was of gray satin scattered over with a design,

---

[18] Blouse

worked in beads, that looked like tiny fish. Her coif was the tall medieval hennin of Plougastel, a flood of lace falling from its summit. Eliane, majestically carried on her white-lace cushion, wore a long robe of lace and lawn, and again I found this very silly, since if by chance she wished to walk, she would certainly stumble in it! The curé was replaced by the bishop of the cathedral, who walked with a tall golden stick, twisted at the top into a pretty design. Papa, who was near me, explained to me that this was called a crozier(*crosse*), which puzzled me, as *crosse* is also the name for the drumstick of a chicken. I also learned that what I called the bishop's hat was a miter. When he passed before us every one knelt down except me, for I wished to gaze with all my eyes at the magnificent apparition. The bishop leaned toward me, smiling, and made a little cross on my forehead with his thumb, and then he put his hand, which was very white and adorned with a great ring of amethyst and diamond, before my lips. "Kiss Monseigneur's hand," papa whispered, and, again much puzzled, I obeyed, for *maman* and *bonne maman* gave their hands to be kissed by men and never kissed theirs. When the bishop put the salt in Eliane's mouth she made the most hideous grimace. Heavens! How ugly she was! *Maman* took her into her arms to calm her. I was near *bonne maman* who had been borne in her sedan-chair into the cathedral, and I whispered to her: "You say that she is pretty, *bonne maman*. Only look at her now! Doesn't she look like an angry little monkey!" But *bonne maman* reminded me in a low voice that unless I was very good, I was not to come to the christening breakfast, and, hastily, I began to turn my tongue in my mouth.

I remember that on this day *bonne maman* had left her puce-color and looked like an old fairy as she sat, covered with all her jewels, in the sedan-chair, dressed in orange-colored velvet.

When we came out of the cathedral the square was full of people, and all the children of Quimper were there. My father, leading me by the hand, was followed by a servant who carried a basket of *dragées*. He took out a bagful and told me that I was to throw them to the children, and this I did with great gusto. What a superb bombardment it was! The children rolled upon the ground, laughed, and howled, while *maman*, and *bonne maman* from the window of her chair, scattered handfuls of *centimes*, *sous*, and *liards*, an old coin of the period that no longer exists. Never in my life have I seen happier children. The accompanied us to our door and stayed for a long time outside in the street, singing Breton canticles and crying, "Vive Mademoiselle Liane!"

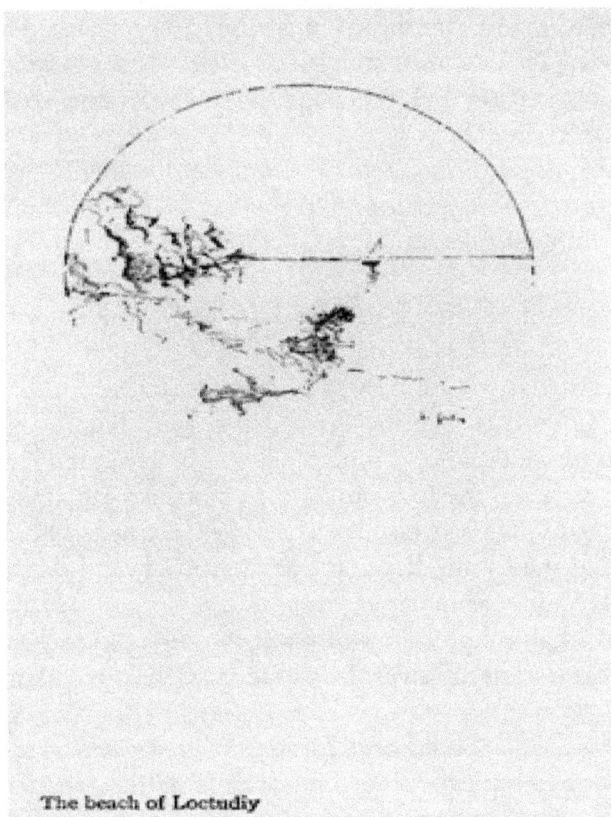

The beach of Loctudiy

The beach of Loctudiy

It must have been at about this time that I first saw the sea and had my first sea-bath. Papa said one day that he would take me to the beach of Loctudiy, near Quimper, with old Gertrude. It is a vast sandy beach, with scattered rocks that, to my childish eyes, stood like giants around us. Gertrude took off my shoes and stockings, and we picked up the shells that lay along the beach in the sunlight like a gigantic rainbow. What a delight it was! Some were white, some yellow, some pink, and some of a lovely rosy mauve. I could not pick them up fast enough or carry those I already had. My little pail overflowed, and the painful problem that confronts all children engaged in this delicious pursuit would soon have oppressed me if my thoughts had not been turned in another direction by the sight of papa making his way toward the sea in bathing-dress. The sea was immense and mysterious, and my beloved papa looked very small before it. I ran to him crying:

"Don't go, papa! Don't go! You will be drowned!"

"There is no danger of that, my pet," said my father. "See how smooth and blue the water is. Don't you want to come with me?"

I felt at once that I did, and in the twinkling of an eye Gertrude had undressed me, my father had me in his arms, and before I could say "Ouf!" I was plunged from head to foot in the Atlantic Ocean. It was my second baptism, and I still feel an agreeable shudder when I remember it. My father held me under the arms to teach me to swim, and I vigorously agitated my little legs and arms. Then I was given back to Gertrude, who dried me and, taking me by the hand, made me run up and down on the hot sand until I was quite warm.

When I came home, full of pride in my exploits, I told *bonne maman* that during my swim I had met a whale which had looked at me.

"And were you afraid of it?" asked *bonne maman*.

"Oh, no," I replied. "They do not eat children. I patted it."

Perhaps my tendency to tell tall stories dates from this time.

CHAPTER III

The Fête at Ker-Eliane

IT was shortly after Eliane's christening, and to celebrate my mother's recovery, that my father gave a great entertainment at Ker-Eliane, near Loch-ar-Brugg.

Loch-ar-Brugg, which means Place of Heather, was an old manor and property that my father had bought and at that time used as a hunting-lodge, and Ker-Eliane was a wild, beautiful piece of country adjoining it, a pleasure resort, called after my mother's name.

To reach Loch-ar-Brugg we all went by the traveling carriage to my father's native town of Landerneau. I dreaded these journeys, since inside the carriage I always became sick; but on this occasion I sat outside near an old servant of my grandmother's called Soisick, the diminutive of François, and was very happy, since in the open air I did not suffer at all. Soisick was an old Breton from Brest. He wore the costume of that part of the country, a tightly fitting, long, black jacket opening over a waistcoat adorned with white-bone buttons, full knee-breeches of coarse, white linen girded over the waistcoat with a red woolen sash, with white woolen stockings, and black shoes. One still sees very old Bretons wearing this costume, but nowadays the peasants prefer the vulgar, commonplace dress of modern work-people.

My father was waiting for us on the quay of Landerneau. What joy I felt when I saw him! When he climbed up beside me and Soisick my happiness was complete.

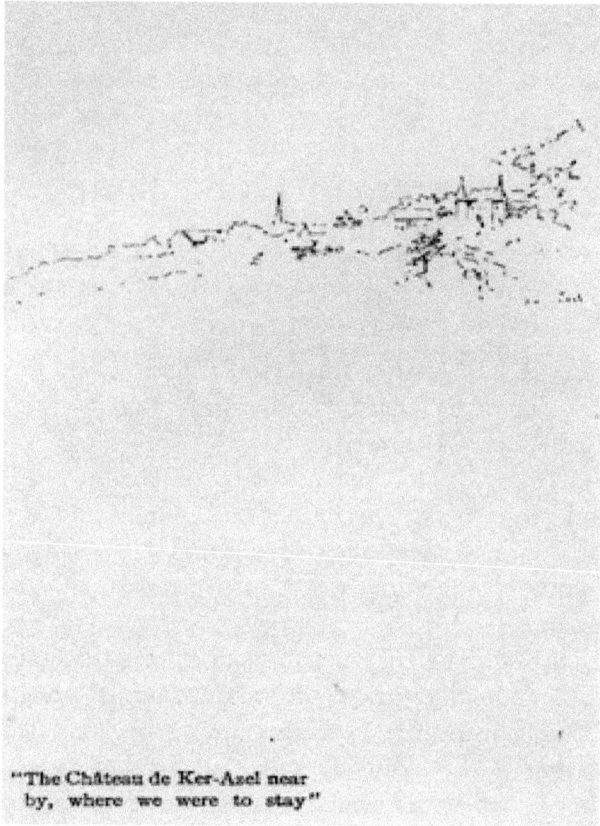

"The Château de Ker-Azel near by, where we were to stay"

"The Château de Ker-Azel nearby, where we were to stay"

Loch-ar-Brugg at that time was not suitably arranged for our habitation, and we drove on to the Château de Ker-Azel nearby, where we were to stay with my *tante* de Laisieu. This elder sister of my mother's was a fat, untidy, shiftless woman who had once been a beauty, but whose abundant fair hair was now faded, and who went about her house and gardens in the mornings *en camisole*. When dressed for the day her appearance was hardly more decorous, for she wore no stays, and fastened the slender bodices of her old dresses across her portly person in a very haphazard fashion, so that intervals of white underclothing showed between the straining hooks. She was a singular contrast to my mother, always so freshly perfect in every detail of her toilet. The château was partly old and partly new and very ugly, though the park that sloped down to it was fine. Near the château stood a very old and beautifully carved font that must have belonged to a church long since destroyed. Later on, in the days of her descendants, it was kept filled with growing flowers and was a beautiful object, but my aunt merely used it as a sort of waste-paper basket for any scraps she picked up in the park. We children used to conceal ourselves in it in our games of hide-and-seek. I enjoyed myself among my many cousins, for I was at this time so young and so naughty that they tended to give way to me in everything. One of them, however, a singularly selfless and devout boy called France, was fond of me for myself, and though I never paid much attention to him, victim rather than playmate as he usually was in the games of others, I was always aware of his gentle, protecting presence, and happy when his peaceful gaze rested upon me. After long years of separation and in our great old age we discovered, France and I, that we had always been dear friends, and in the few years that remained to us before his recent death we saw each other constantly. But I must return to the fête.

My mother and my aunt were absorbed in preparations. It was a general hurly-burly, every one running north, south, east, and west–to Landerneau, to Morlaix, to Brest, to every place, in short, that could boast some special delicacy. And at last the great day came, and we children were up with the lark. There was first to be a luncheon for the huntsmen, friends of papa's, and the ladies were to follow in carriages and to enter Ker-Eliane from the highroad. But we preferred the shorter way, by the deep paths overgrown with hawthorn and blackberry. The boys rushed along on the tops of the *talus*, the sort of steep bank that in Brittany takes the place of hedges, and even with Jeannie to restrain me I was nearly as torn and tattered as they when we arrived at Ker-Eliane. What a fairy-land it was! Rocks and streams, heathery hills, and woods full of bracken. An old ruin, strange and melancholy, with only a few crumbling walls and a portion of ivy-clothed tower left standing, rose among trees on a little hill near the entrance, and farther on, surrounded by woods of beech or pine, were three lakes, lying in a chain one after the other. Water-lilies grew upon them and at their brinks a pinkish-purple flower the name of which I never knew. The third lake was so somber and mysterious that my father had called it the Styx. An ancient laurel-tree–in Brittany the laurels become immense trees–had been uprooted in a thunderstorm and had fallen across the Styx, making a natural rustic bridge. We children were forbidden to cross on it, but on this day I remember my adventurous cousin Jules rushing to and fro from one bank to the other in defiance of authority. At the foot of the hill, below the ruin, a clear, delicious stream sprang forth from a stony cleft and wound through a valley and out into the lower meadows, and at the entrance to the valley, among heather and enormous mossy rocks, rose a cross of gray stone without Christ or ornaments. The peasants made pilgrimages to it on Good Friday, but I never learned its history.

It was among the lower meadows, in a charming, smiling spot planted with chestnuts, poplars, and copper beeches, that the table for the thirty huntsmen was laid in the shade of a little avenue. Already the *crêpe* -makers from Quimper, renowned through all the country, were laying their fires upon the ground under the trees, and I must pause here to describe this Breton dish. A carefully compounded batter, flavored either with vanilla or malaga, was ladled upon a large flat pan and spread thinly out to its edge with a wooden implement rather like a paper-cutter. By means of this knife the *crêpes*, when browned on one side, were turned to the other with a marvelous dexterity, then lifted from the pan and folded at once into a square, like a pocket-handkerchief, for, if allowed to cool, they cracked. They were as fine as paper–six would have made the thickness of an ordinary pancake, and were served very hot with melted butter and fresh cream, of which a crystal jar stood before each guest, and was replenished by the servants as it was emptied.

"A feast was spread at a little distance
from the peasants, and wine flowed all day"

"A feast was spread at a little distance from the peasants, and wine flowed all day"

The *crêpes* were eaten at the end of the luncheon as a sweet, and among the other dishes that I remember was the cold salmon,–invariable on such occasions, salmon abounding in our Breton rivers,–with a highly spiced local sauce, *filet de boeuf en aspic*, York ham, fowls, Russian salad, and the usual cakes and fruits. The huntsmen seated at this feast did not wear the pink coast and top-hats of more formal occasions, but dark jackets and knee-breeches and the small, round Breton cap with upturned brim that admitted of a pipe being tucked into it at one side. And so they carried their pipes, as the peasants did, and the legitimists among them had a golden fleur-de-lis fixed in front. The ladies of the party, in summer dresses and wide-brimmed hats, arrived when the more substantial part of the repast was over, and their carriages filled the highroad outside the precincts of Ker-Eliane. A feast was spread at a little distance for the peasants, and wine flowed all day. After the feasting, two famous *biniou*[19]-players took up their places on the high *talus*[20] that separated Ker-Eliane from Loch-ar-Brugg and played the *farandol*, the *jabadao*, and other country-dances for the peasants to dance to. The *biniou* is rather like a small bagpipe and produces a wild, shrill sound. The players wore a special costume: their caps and their stockings were bright red; their jackets and waistcoat bright blue, beautifully embroidered; their full white breeches of coarse linen. Like all the peasants at that time, they wore their hair long, falling over the shoulders. It was a charming sight to see the peasants dancing, all in their local costumes. The women's skirts were of black or red stuff, with three bands of velvet, their bodices of embroidered velvet, and they all wore a gold or silver Breton cross, hung on a black velvet ribbon, round their necks, and a *Saint Esprit* embroidered in gold on the front of their bodices. Among the coifs I remember several beautiful tall hennins. What a day it was! Landerneau talked of it for years, and I have never forgotten it. We children had our luncheon sitting on the grass near the big table, and afterward there were endless games among the heather and bracken. My little sister Elaine appeared, carried in her pink basket, and seemed to look about her with great approval.

Later on in the day, when the dancing had begun, we went to look on at that, and I wanted very much to dance, too; but nobody asked me, for I was too little. I must by that time have begun to get very tired and troublesome, for I remember that *maman* promised me a little wheelbarrow if I would be good and allowed Jeannie to take me back to Ker-Azel. I was already sleepy, as I had drunk a quantity of champagne, with which the servants had replenished my little liqueur-glass, and I allowed myself at last to be carried away by Jeannie, and fell asleep in her arms.

---

[19] Breton bagpipes
[20] Embankment

"In the panels of the great oaken
door . . . were little grated squares"

*"In the panels of the great oaken door...
were little grated squares"*

CHAPTER IV

The Old House at Landerneau

URING these early years of my life our time, though mainly spent with *bonne maman* at Quimper, was also given for many months of the year to Landerneau, and a little later on was divided between these two houses and Loch-ar-Brugg. At Landerneau we lived in a vast old house that had been part of my mother's marriage dowry. The family house, equally old and vast, of the Kerouguets was also at Landerneau, and the house of dear Tante Rose, my father's eldest sister. Landerneau was a picturesque old town, so near the sea that the tides rose and fell in the River Elorn, which flowed through it. A legend ran that the part of Landerneau lying on the southern banks of the river, still all wild with great rocks that seemed to have been hurled together by some giant's hand, had been reduced to this condition by the devil. He had been traveling through the country, and the inhabitants of the southern half of Landerneau had refused to give him food and drink, whereas those of the northern half had suitably and diplomatically entertained him; and it was in vengeance that he had hurled these great rocks across the river, to remain as permanent, if picturesque, embarrassments to southern Landerneau. The morality of the story was disconcerting, and very much puzzled me when I was told it by old Gertrude. Our house formed a corner of the principal street in the northern side of the town. In the days of the Terror, not so far distant in my childhood, it had been used, with the house of Tante Rose across the way, as a prison where the condemned were put on their way to be guillotined at Brest, and a subterranean passage that ran between the two houses, under the street, conveyed the unfortunates swiftly and unobtrusively, if occasion required it, from one prison to the other. Another lugubrious memento of that terrible time were the small square openings in the floors of the upper rooms in these houses. In our days they were used to summon servants from below, but their original purpose had been for watching the captives unobserved. In the panels of the great oaken door that opened on the street, in our house, were little grated squares through which those who knocked for admittance could be cautiously examined, and this feature gave a further idea of the strange and perilous circumstances of bygone days. The kitchen, which was entered from a stone hall, was our delight; it was called the every-day kitchen. Enormous logs burned in a vast open fireplace, archaically carved. At that time coal was little known in the country, and the joints were roasted on a spit before this fire, which looked like the entrance to an inferno. There was a little oven for stews and sweets, etc. Under a square glass case on the mantel-shelf, lifted high above the busy scene, stood a statue of the Virgin, very old and very ugly, dressed in tinsel, a necklace of colored beads around its neck. This was a cherished possession of Nicole's, an old cook of my grandmother's, who followed us everywhere, and at its foot, under the glass cover, lay her withered orange-flower wedding-wreath. The kitchen was lighted at night by numbers of tallow candles that burned in tall brass candlesticks, each with its pincers and snuffer. (A candle with us does not "take snuff"; it has "its nose blown"—*on mouchait la chandelle.*) Brass warming-pans, which we children called Bluebeard's wives, were ranged along the walls, and a multitude of copper saucepans hung in order of size, glittering with special splendor on those spaces that could be seen from the street, for "*où l'orgueil ne va t'il pas se nicher?*"[21] Through an opening in the wall opposite the big windows dishes could be passed to the servants in the dining-room during meals.

---

[21] Where the pride goes to nest.

"In the days of the Terror . . . it had been used . . . as a prison"

"In the days of the Terror ... it had been used ... as a prison"

The dining-room windows looked out at a garden full of flowers, the high walls embroidered with espalier fruit-trees, plum-, cherry-, mulberry-, and medlar-trees growing along the paths. At the bottom of the garden was a large aviary containing golden and silver pheasants, magpies, canaries, and exotic birds that my father's naval friends had brought him from their long Oriental voyages. My father himself tended these birds, and I can answer for it that they lacked nothing. I must tell here of the strange behavior of a golden pheasant. Despite papa's gentleness and care, this bird seemed to detest him and would not let him enter the aviary; but when I came with papa, the pheasant would run to the wires and eat the bread I held out to it from my hand.

Papa was surprised and interested, and suggested one day that I should go with him into the aviary and "see what the pheasant would say." No sooner said than done. The bird rushed at papa and pecked at his feet with a singular ferocity; then, feeling, evidently, that he had disposed of his enemy, he turned to me, spread out his wings before me, bowed up and down as if an ecstasy of reverent delight, and taking the bread I held out to him, he paid no more attention at all to papa.

The principal rooms on the ground floor of the house opened on a stone hall with an inlaid marble floor, where, in a niche carved in the wall, and facing the wide stone staircase, stood another Virgin, much larger and even older than Nicole's. She was of stone, with a blunted, gentle countenance, and hands held out at each side in a graceful, simple gesture that seemed to express surprise as much as benediction. As we came down from our rooms every morning it was as if she greeted us always with a renewed interest. Fresh flowers were laid at her feet every day, and we were all taught, the boys to lift their hats, the girls to drop deep curtseys before her. Indeed, these respects were paid by us to all the many statues of the Virgin that are seen on our Breton roads. From the hall one entered the salon, with its inlaid parquet floor, so polished that we were forbidden to slide upon it, for it was as slippery as ice, and falls were inevitable for disobedient children. On the mantelpiece was a clock representing Marius weeping over the ruins of Carthage. His cloak lay about his knees, and we used to feel that he would have done much better had he drawn it up and covered his chilly-looking bronze shoulders. On each side of the clock were white vases with garlands in relief upon them of blue convolvulus and their green leaves. But what bewitched us children were the big Chinese porcelain figures, mandarins sitting cross-legged, with heads that nodded gently up and down at the slightest movement made in the room. Their bellies were bare, their eyes seemed to laugh, and they were putting out their tongues. Black ibises upon their robes opened wide beaks to catch butterflies. I remember crossing the hall on tiptoe and opening the salon-door very softly and looking in at the mandarins sitting there in their still merriment; and it required a little courage, as though one summoned a spell, to shake the door and rouse them into life. The heads gently nodded, the eyes seemed to laugh with a new meaning at me now; and I gazed, half frightened, half laughing, too, until all again was motionless. It was as if a secret jest had passed between me and the mandarins. In an immense room to the left of the salon that had once, perhaps, been a ball-room, but was now used as a laundry, was a high sculptured fireplace that was my joy. On each side the great greyhounds, sitting up on their hind legs, sustained the mantelpiece, all garlanded with vines. Among the leaves and grapes one saw a nest of little birds, with their beaks wide open, and the father and mother perched above them. And, most beautiful of all, a swallow in flight only touched with the tip of a wing a leaf, and really seemed to be flying. Only my father appreciated this masterpiece, which must have been a superb example of Renaissance work, and when, years afterward, my mother sold the house, the new owner had it broken up and carted away because it took up too much room!

On the two floors above were many bedrooms not only for our growing family, but for that of my Aunt de Laisieu, who, with all her children, used to pay us long and frequent visits, so that even in the babyhood of Eliane and Ernest and Maraquita I never lacked companionship.

My mother's room was called *la chambre des colonnes*, because at the foot of the bed, and used there instead of bedposts, were two great stone pillars wreathed with carving and reaching to the ceiling. What a pretty room it was! In spring its windows looked down at a sea of fruit-blossoms and flowers in the garden beneath. The bed had a domed canopy, with white muslin curtains embroidered in green spots. Above the doors were two allegorical paintings, one of Love, who makes Time pass, and one of Time, who makes Love pass. A deep, mysterious drawer above the oaken mantelpiece was used by *maman* for storing pots of especially exquisite preserves that were kept for winter use. On her dressing-table, flowing with muslin and ribbons, I specially remember the great jar of *eau de Cologne*, which one used to buy, as if it were wine, by the liter.

From this room led papa's, more severe and masculine. Here there were glass cabinets fitted on each side into the deep window-seats and containing bibelots from all over the world. A group of family miniatures hung on the wall near the fireplace.

On a turning of the staircase was a bath-room, with a little sort of sentry-box for cold douches, and at the top of the house an enormous garret, filled with broken old spinning-wheels and furniture, bundles of old dresses, chests full of dusty papers. I found here one day *bonne maman's* betrothal-dress. It was of stiff, rich satin, a wide blue and white stripe, with a dark line on each side of the blue and a little garland of pink roses running up the white. The long, pointed bodice was incredibly narrow. A strange detail was the coarseness with which this beautiful dress was finished inside. It was lined with a sort of sacking, and the old lace with which it was still adorned was pinned into place with brass safety-pins. Finally, for my description of the house, there was a big courtyard, with the servants' quarters built round it, and a clear little stream ran through a *basse-cour* stocked with poultry.

I had not seen this house for over fifty years when, some time ago, I went to visit it. The new proprietor, an unprepossessing person, was leaning against the great oaken door. He permitted me, very ungraciously, to enter.

I went through all these rooms that two generations ago had rung with the sounds of our happy young life, and it was misery to me. In the kitchen, which had been so beautiful, the window-panes were broken, and the dismantled walls daubed with whitewash, with dusty, empty bottles where Nicole's Virgin had stood. Upon the table was a greasy, discolored oil-cloth, where one saw M. Thiers, with knitted eyebrows and folded arms, surrounded by tricolor flags. The salon—I sobbed as I stood and looked about it; all, all that I had known and loved had disappeared. The stone Virgin was gone from her niche in the hall. Trembling, I mounted to my dear parents' rooms. What desolation! Unmade beds and rickety iron bedsteads; dust, disorder, and dirt. The carved chimneypiece, with its great drawer, was gone; the paper was peeled from the walls. Only over the doors, almost invisible under their cobwebs, were the painted panels of Love, who makes Time pass, and Time, who makes Love pass. The garden was a dung-heap.

When I came out, pale and shaken, the proprietor, still complacently leaning against the door, remarked, "*Eh bien*, Madam is glad to have seen her house, isn't she!"

The animal! I could have strangled him!

"I felt that Tante Rose was enchanting"

"I felt that Tante Rose was enchanting"

CHAPTER V

Tante Rose

OVER the way lived Tante Rose. We children liked best to go to her house by means of the subterranean passage. It was pitch-dark, and we felt a fearful delight as we galloped through it at full speed, and then beat loudly upon the door at the other end, so that old Kerandraon should not keep us waiting for a moment in the blackness. In the salon, between the windows, her tame magpie hopping near her, we would find Tante Rose spinning at her wheel. There were pink ribbons on her distaff, and her beautiful, rounded arms moved gently to and fro drawing out the fine white linen thread. Sitting, as I see her thus, with her back to the light, her white tulle head-dress and the tulle bow beneath her chin surrounded her delicate, rosy face with a sort of aureole. She had a pointed little chin and gay, blue eyes, and though she had snowy hair, she looked so young and was so active that she seemed to have quicksilver in her veins. A tranquil mirth was her distinguishing characteristics, and even when hardly more than a baby I felt that Tante Rose was enchanting. Her first question was sure to be, "Are you hungry?" and even if we had just risen from a meal we were sure to be hungry when we came to see Tante Rose. She would blow into a little silver whistle that hung at her waist, and old Kerandraon (we children pronounced it Ker-le dragon) would appear with his benevolent, smiling face.

"Take Mademoiselle Sophie's orders, Kerandraon," Tante Rose would say; but the dear old man, who was a great friend, did not need to wait for them.

"Demoiselle would like *crêpes* and fresh cream; and there is the rest of the chocolate paste which Demoiselle likes, too."

Old Kerandraon

Old Kerandraon

"Bring what pleases you," Tante Rose would say, "and take my key, Kerandraon, and fetch the box of *sucre d'orge*[22] from the shelf in my wardrobe." When Kerandraon had come ambling back with his laden tray he would stop and talk with us while we ate. He was seventy years old and had a noble air in his long Louis XV jacket. Tante Rose's mother had taken him from the streets when he was a little beggar-boy of twelve. He lived in the family service all his life, and when he died at seventy-five he was buried in the family vault. Jacquette, the magpie, sometimes

---

[22] Rock candy

became very noisy on these festive occasions, and Tante Rose would say: "Go into the garden, Jacquette. *Tu m'annuis* "(so she pronounced *ennuies*). And Jacquette, who seemed to understand everything she said, would go obediently hopping off. In the garden, adjoining the salon, was a greenhouse full of grapes and flowers, and that was another haven of delight on our visits to Tante Rose. It was the prettiest sight to see her mounted on a step-ladder cutting the grapes. A servant held the ladder, and another the basket into which the carefully chosen bunches were dropped. Tante Rose's little feet were shod in a sort of high-heeled brown-satin slipper called *cothurnes*, probably because they tied in classic fashion across the instep, little gold acorns hanging at the ends of the ribbons. I have the most distinct recollection of these exquisite feet as I stood beside the ladder looking up at Tante Rose and waiting for her to drop softly a great bunch of grapes into my hands. The fruit-trees of Tante Rose's garden were famous. A great old fig-tree there was so laden with fruit that supports had to be put under the heavy branches; there were wonderful Smyrna plums, and an apple-tree covered with tiny red apples that were our joy. From a high terrace in the garden one could watch all that went on in the town below. Tante Rose's cream, too, was famous. Great earthenware pans of milk stood on the wide shelves of her dairy, and when *maman* came to see her she would say, "May I go into the dairy, Rose?" It was always known what this meant. *Maman* would skim for herself a bowlful of the thick, golden cream.

"She did not conceal that she found him a dull companion"

"She did not conceal that she found him a dull companion"

Even the kitchen had an elegance, a grace, and sparkle all its own, and it is here that I can most characteristically see Tante Rose distributing milk for the poor of Landerneau. Her farmers' wives had brought it in from the country in large, covered pails, and Tante Rose, dressed in a morning-gown of puce, colored silk (like *bonne maman* in this, she wore no other color), her full sleeves, with their wide lawn cuffs turned back over her arms, ladled it into jars, giving her directions the while to the servants: "This for Yann. This for Hervé [an old cripple]. Did this milk come from the yellow? It is sure, then, to be very good; take it to the hospital and—wait! This little jug of cream to the *supérieure*; she is so fond of it. And, Laic, this large jar is for the prison," for Tante Rose forgot nobody, and all with such quiet grace and order. The poor of Landerneau adored her. The thread she spun was woven at her country place, La Fontaine Blanche, into linen to make clothes for them, and she knitted socks and waistcoats even as she went about the streets on her errands of mercy. If the poor loved her, it was respect mingled with a little fear that the *bourgeoisie* felt, for she had no patience with scandal-mongering and sharply checked their gossiping, provincial habits. The chatelaines of the surrounding country sought her out and delighted in her charm, her accomplishments, and her devil-may-care wit. Tante Rose was married to a wealthy and excellent Landernean, Joseph Goury, whom we called Tonton Joson, and his friends, Jason. He had a placid, kindly face, and stout, fine calves incased in silk stockings. Still in love with his wife, he was patiently submissive to her gay sallies; for though very fond of him, she did not conceal that she found him a dull companion. Very drolly, though she tutoyéd[23] him, she used always to address him as "Monsieur Goury." "*Tais-toi[24], Monsieur Goury,*" she would say; "you are as tiresome as the flies." And after enduring his prosy talk for some time she would say quite calmly: "I am beginning to drink hemlock. Go away, Monsieur Goury—*va t'en.* You bore me to distraction. You stun and stupefy me. Go away. *Je n'en puis plus.*" And poor Tonton Joson remaining helplessly gazing, she would lift the little trap-door beside her chair, if the scene took place in her room, and call out to the servants below, "Tell Liac to come up and help monsieur on with his coat."

"But, my dear, I was not thinking of going out," Tonton Joson would protest; and Tante Rose would reply:

"*Mais tu sors, Monsieur Goury.*"

Tante Rose was very devout, but after her own fashion. She read the office to herself every day, but had many *librepensant*[25] friends, with whom she used good-temperedly to argue. Any bishop who came to Landerneau stayed always with Tante Rose.

Her cuisine was the best I have ever eaten; and oh, the incredible abundance of those days! All the courses were served at once upon the immense table. The great silver soup-tureen, big enough for a baby's bath, and so tall that she had to stand up to it, was in front of Tante Rose, and before she began to ladle

---

[23] Call someone 'tu'
[24] Be quiet
[25] Free thinking

out the platefuls, with the light, accurate movements of her arms characteristic of her, a servant carefully fastened behind her long sleeves *à la pagode*. It was really charming to watch her serving the soup, and I remember one guest asserting that he would eat *potage* four times if Mme. Goury helped him to it.

An enormous salmon usually occupied the center of the table, and there were six *entrées*, four *rôtis*, two hot and two cold, and various *entremets* and desserts. A favorite *entrée* was a *purée* of pistachio nuts, with roasted sheeps' tails on silver spits stuck into it. The hot dishes stood on silver heaters filled with glowing charcoal. Between the courses little pots of cream, chocolate, vanilla, and coffee were actually passed and actually eaten! Chocolate cream to fill the gap between woodcock and *foie-gras*, for instance! Champagne-bottles stood in silver coolers at each corner of the table. I wonder that we all survived. On the other hand, when Tante Rose or my mother received the visits of their friends, there was no afternoon tea to offer them, as nowadays. The servants merely passed round little glasses of Spanish wines and plates of small biscuits. The good ladies of Landerneau afforded, I imagine, much amusement to my mother and to Tante Rose, who, though a native, was of a very different caliber. One little trait I remember was very illustrative of the bourgeois habit of mind. At that time, as now, lengths of velvet were included in every *corbeille* offered to a bride by the bridegroom's family, and the velvet dresses made from them were dignified institutions worn year after year. One knows how marked and unsightly velvet soon becomes if sat upon, and it was a wise and crafty fashion to have a breadth of perfectly matching silk introduced between the full folds at the back of these dresses, so that when one sat down it was upon the silk. It was in regard to this sensible contrivance that the ladies of Landerneau were reported to declare that it was strange indeed to see the *noblesse* so miserly that they could not afford a whole velvet dress, and therefore let silk into the back.

Some of Tante Rose's children were, like herself, very clever and charming, some very stupid, like Tonton Joson. It can be imagined what games we all had. Once, in the coach-house, my older cousins put young Raoul into a large basket with a number of smooth stones under him and told him that they were eggs and that if he were quiet and patient, they would hatch out. Then by means of a rope and pulley to which the basket was attached (it must have been used for raising and lowering hay and fodder) we pulled poor Raoul up to the rafters, and there we left him and forgot all about him. His desolate cries were heard after a time, and when he was rescued, it was found that the rocking of the basket had made him very seasick.

"I had only to sweep up the rubbish . . . and carry it out of the wood in my little wheelbarrow"

"I had only to sweep up the rubbish... and carry it out of the wood in my little wheelbarrow"

Of all our games the best were those in the woods of La Fontaine Blanche. This property of Tante Rose's, with its old manor-house dating from the time of Queen Anne of Brittany, was near Landerneau, and since papa went there nearly every day, caring for it as if it were his own, we were able to go with him and take full possession of the beautiful woods. We were given planks and tools, and we built a little hut on the banks of the stream. I was so young that my share of the labors was unexacting, as I had only to sweep up the rubbish left by the builders and carry it out of the wood in my little wheelbarrow; but I remember that pride with which I felt myself associated in any capacity with such marvels of construction. Not only was the hut entirely built by my cousins, but they made an oven inside it and even fabricated a sort of earthenware service with the clay soil found along the banks of the stream. It would never fire properly, however, and therefore our attempts to bake bread were not successful.

But *crêpes*, as pure-blooded young Bretons, we could make, and our parents were often entertained by us and regaled with them as they sat under the trees. Oh, how happy we were! The woods were full of lilies of the valley, and our hut had been baptized by the curé of Landerneau the château de la Muguetterie, while we were called *Robinson Crusoes*, and this was to us all our greatest glory.

CHAPTER VI

The Demoiselles de Coatnamprun

ACROSS the way from our house in Landerneau lived two old maiden ladies, the Demoiselles de Coatnamprun. The Marquis and Marquise de Coatnamprun, their father and mother, had died many years ago, and most of the small fortune had been filched from them in some iniquitous lawsuit. I remember them very clearly, for I often went to see them with *maman* and Tante Rose, who watched over them and protected them; gentle, austere figures, dressed always in threadbare black, almost like nuns, with long, white bone rosaries hanging at their sides, and on their breasts, tied with a red cord, great crucifixes of brass and wood. Around their necks they wore white handkerchiefs folded, the points behind, and when they went out, old-fashioned black *capotes*, which were large bonnets, mounted and drawn on wires, a quilling of white inside around the face. The elder was called Isménie, and the younger Suzette; they had the tenderest love for each other.

Their house was one of the oldest in Landerneau and was covered with strange carvings. The great knocker always fascinated me, for it represented a devil with his pitchfork, and one lifted the pitchfork to knock. Almost always it was one of the Demoiselles de Coatnamprun who answered, and she always held a clean white handkerchief by the center, the points shaken out, and always swept us, as she appeared before us in the doorway, a wonderful, old-fashioned, stately court curtsey. The sisters were plain, with dark, mild eyes, faded skins, and pale, withered lips; but their teeth were beautiful, and they had abundant hair. Isménie's features were harsh, and her half-closed, near-sighted eyes gave her a cold and haughty expression;

53

but in reality she was a lamb of gentleness, and no one seeing the sisters in their poverty would have taken them for anything but *grandes dames.*

"Gentle, austere figures, dressed
always in threadbare black"

"Gentle, austere figures, dressed always in threadbare black"

When we were ushered into the house it was usually into the dining-room that we went. The drawing-room, which was called the *salle de compagnie,* was used only on ceremonious occasions, Easter, the bishop's visit, or when the *noblesse* from the surrounding country called, and the proudest among them were proud to do so. So in the *salle de compagnie*, where engravings of the family coats of arms hung along the walls, the ugly, massive mahogany furniture was usually shrouded in cotton covers, and it was in the dining-room that the sisters sat, making clothes for the poor. Here the pictures interested me very much; they were *naif*, brightly colored prints bought at the Landerneau fairs, and representing events in the lives of the saints. St. Christopher, bending with his staff in the turbulent stream, bore on his shoulder a child so tiny that I could never imagine why its weight should incommode him, and another doll-like child stood on the volume held by St. Anthony of Padua. The oilcloth cover on the table had all the kings and queens of France marching in procession round its border, the dates of their reigns printed above their heads. The chairs were common straw-bottomed kitchen chairs. *Maman* sometimes tried to persuade the sisters to paint the chairs, saying that if they were painted bright red, for instance, it would make the room so much more cheerful. But to any such suggestion they would reply, with an air of gentle surprise: "Oh, but *maman* had them like that. We can't change anything that *maman* had." Their large bedroom was on the first floor, looking out at the street. It was a most dismal room. The two four-posted beds, side by side, had canopies and curtains of old tapestry, but this was all covered with black cambric muslin and had the most funeral air imaginable. At the head of Isménie's bed, crossed against the black, were two bones that she had brought from the family vault on some occasion when the coffins had been moved or opened. The only cheerful thing I remember was a childish little *étagère*[26] fastened in a corner and filled with the waxen figures of the *petit Jésus* and the tiny china dogs, cats and birds that had been among their presents on Christmas mornings. To give an idea of the extreme simplicity and innocence of the Demoiselles de Coatnamprun I may say here that to the end of their lives they firmly believed that *le petit Jésus* himself came down their kitchen chimney on Christmas Eve and left their presents for them on the kitchen table. *Le petit Jésus*, as a matter of fact, was on these occasions impersonated by

---

[26] Shelf

maman and Tante Rose. Tante Rose always had the key of the sisters' house, so that at any time she could go in and see that nothing was amiss with *ses enfants*, as she tenderly called them,– and indeed to the end they remained lovely and ingenuous children,–so she and *maman*, when the sisters were safely asleep, would steal into the house and pile every sort of good thing, from legs of mutton to *galettes*, upon the table, and fill the garden sabots that stood ready with bonbons, handkerchiefs, and the little china figures of animals the sisters so cherished. And always there was a waxen figure of *le petit Jésus* and the card with which he made his intention clear; for "*Aux Demoiselles de Coatnamprun, du petit Jésus* " was written upon it.

Other instances of the sisters' ignorance of life and the world I might give, but they would simply be received with incredulity. Such types no longer exist, and even then the sisters were unique. I do not believe that in all their lives they knew an evil thought; they were incapable of any form of envy or malice or uncharitableness, and filled with delight at any good fortune that came to others and with gratitude for their own lot in life. Sometimes Suzette, in the intimacy of friends, would refer with simple sadness to the one drama, if such it can be called, that had befallen them. "*Oui*," she would say, "*Isménie a eu un chagrin d'amour*." Once, when they were young, in their parents' lifetime, an officer had been quartered with them, a kindly, intelligent, honest young fellow of the *bourgeoisie*, and at once aware of the atmosphere of distinction that surrounded him. He showed every attention to the sisters, and poor Isménie found him altogether charming. He never even guessed at her attachment. Indeed, no such a marriage at that time would have been possible, but she was broken-hearted when he went away. Her sister was her confidante, and this was the *chagrin d'amour*[27] to which Suzette sometimes referred.

I have said that when they walked out they wore *capotes*. On one occasion Mlle. Suzette found in a drawer, among old rubbish put away, a crumpled artificial rose, a pink rose, and had the strange idea of fastening it in front of her *capote*. Isménie,

---

[27] Sorrow of love

when her near-sighted eyes caught sight of it, stopped short in the street and peered at her sister in astonishment. "But, Suzette, what have you there?" she asked. Suzette bashfully told her that she had found the rose and thought it might look pretty. "No, no," said Isménie, turning with her sister back to the house, "you must not wear it. *Maman* never wore anything in her *capote*." It required all my mother's skill to persuade them to allow her to dress their hair for them on the occasion of an evening party at Tante Rose's, to which, as usual, they were going, as "maman " had gone, wearing black-lace caps. "*Voyons*, but you have such pretty hair," said *maman*. "Let me only show you how charmingly it can be done." They were tempted, yet uncertain and very anxious, and then *maman* had the opportune memory of an old picture of the marquise in youth, her hair done in puffs upon her forehead. She brought it out triumphantly, and the sisters yielded. They could consent to have their hair done as "*maman's* " had been done in her youth.

We children always went with our parents to the evening parties in Landerneau. *Maman* did not like to leave us, and it will be remembered that in those days one dined at five o'clock and that we children had all our meals except breakfast with our parents. It was at a dinner-party at Tante Rose's that Mlle. Suzette, next whom I sat, said to me smiling, with her shy dignity, "I have a present here for a little girl who has been good," and she drew a small paper parcel from the silk reticule that hung beside the rosary at her side. I opened it, and found, to my delight, a sugar mouse and a tiny pipe made of red sugar such as I knew *maman* would never allow us to eat when we went to the confectioner's. But here, in the presence of Mlle. Suzette, and the gift a gift from her, I felt that I was safe, and I devoured the mouse and pipe at once, quite aware of *maman's* amused and rallying glance from across the table. "I saw you," she said to me afterward. "Little ne'er-do-well, you know that I could not forbid it when Mademoiselle Suzette was there!"

The only flower that grew in the Demoiselles de Coatnamprun's garden was heliotrope, for that had been "*maman's*" favorite flower. They were poor gardeners, and the little *bonne* who came in by the day to do the housework could give them no help in the garden. So it was Tante Rose, trotting on her high heels, a little garden fork on her shoulder, who appeared to do battle with the moss and dandelions and to restore a little order. She always gave to this service the air of a delightful game, and indeed, in her constant care of the poor old ladies, had the prettiest skill imaginable in making her gifts weigh nothing.

"My dears," she would say, leaning forward to look at their black robes, "aren't these dresses getting rather shabby? Hasn't the time come for new ones?"

"They are shabby," Isménie would answer sadly, "but *que voulez-vous, chère Madame*, our means, as you know, are so narrow. It costs so much to buy a dress. We could hardly afford new ones now."

"But, on the contrary, it doesn't cost so much," Tante Rose would say. "I know some excellent woolen material, the very thing for your dresses, and only five francs for the length. You can well afford that, can't you? So I'll buy it for you and bring it tomorrow."

And so she would, the innocent sisters imagining five francs the price of material for which Tante Rose paid at least thirty. Since the sisters were very proud, for all their gentleness, and could consent to accept nothing in the nature of a charity, and since indeed they could hardly have lived at all on what they had, Tante Rose had woven a far-reaching conspiracy about them. Her trades-people had orders to sell their meat and vegetables to the Demoiselles de Coatnamprun at about a fifth of their value. Packets of coffee and sugar arrived at their door, and milk and cream every morning, and when they asked the messenger what the price might be, he would say: "*Ces dames régleront le compte avec Monsieur le Curé,*" and since they did not like to refuse gifts from the curé, the innocent plot was never discovered. Of course fruits from Tante Rose's garden and cakes from her kitchen were things that could be accepted. She would bring them herself, and have a slice of *galette* or a fig from the big basketful with them. They were rather greedy, poor darlings, and since any money they could save went to the poor, they could never buy such dainties for themselves. One extravagance, however, they had:

when they came out to pay a visit, a piece of knitting was always drawn from the reticule, and when one asked what it was one was told in a whisper: "Silk stockings—a Christmas present for Suzette," or Isménie, as the case might be. Beautifully knitted, fine, openwork stockings they were.

Another contrivance for their comfort was invented by Tante Rose. They were great cowards, afraid of the dark and in deadly fear of the possible robbers that might enter their house at night. Tante Rose arranged that when they went to bed a lighted, shaded lamp should be placed in their window, the shade turned toward their room, the light toward the street, so that any robbers passing by would be deceived into thinking the house still on foot and forego their schemes for breaking in.

Their hearts were tender toward all forms of life. I can see one of them rising from her work to rescue a fly that had fallen into trouble and, holding it delicately by the wings, lift the *persiennes* to let it fly away. One day in their garden I cried out in disgust at the sight of a great earthworm writhing across a border.

"Oh, the horrid worm! Quick! A trowel, Mademoiselle, to cut it in two."

But Mademoiselle Suzette came to look with grieved eyes.

"And why kill the poor creature, Sophie? It does us no harm," she said, and helped the worm to disappear in the soft earth.

The Demoiselles de Coatnamprun died one winter of some pulmonary affection and within a day of one another. They died with the simplicity and sincerity that had marked all their lives, and toward the end they were heard to murmur continually, while they smiled as if in sleep, "*Maman—Papa.*"

Isménie died first; but since it was seen that Suzette had only a few hours to live, the body was kept lying on the bed near hers, and she did not know that her beloved sister had been taken from her. They were buried together on the same day.

"They were buried together on the same day"

"They were buried together on the same day"

There was another and very different old lady in Landerneau of whom I was very fond and whom, since she took a great fancy to me, I saw often. Her daughter was a friend of *maman's* and made a *mésalliance*[28] that caused the doors of Landerneau to close upon her. *Maman*, however, remained devoted to her, and continued to see as much of her as ever, and her mother, my old friend, was entirely indifferent to the doors, closed or open, of Landerneau. She wore a brightly colored Turkish silk handkerchief tied turban-wise about her head, and soft gray-leather riding boots,–men's boots,–so that she was known in her quarter as *Chat-botté*. In her own house she wore men's dress-

[28] A marriage with a person of inferior social status

breeches, short jacket, and high boots. Her feet were remarkably small, and the wave of hair on her forehead was as black as jet. She was very downright and ready of speech, and used to talk to me as though I were a person of her own age. "Do you see, Sophie," she would say, "my poor daughter is a great goose. She struggles to be received, and gets only buffets for her pains. Why give oneself so much trouble for nothing?"

The disconsolate daughter and the son-in-law made their home with her in a great old house standing on the banks of the river. He was a wholesale wine merchant, and barrels and casks of wine stood about the entrance. My old friend lived almost entirely in her own room on the first floor, the strangest room. It was at once spotlessly clean and completely untidy. The bed had no posts or canopy and was shaped like a cradle. Bottles of salad-oil stood on the mantel-shelf, and a bunch of carrots might be lying on the table among bundles of newspapers. From the windows one had beautiful views up and down the river and could see the stone bridge that had old houses built upon it. Across the river were her gardens, and she used often to row me over to them and to show me the immense old cherry-tree, planted by her grandfather, that grew far down the river against the walls of an old tower. This tower had its story, and I could not sleep at night for thinking of it. In her girlhood mad people were shut up there. There was only a dungeon-room, and the water often rose in it so that the forsaken creatures stood up to their knees in water. Food was thrown to them through the iron bars of the windows, but it was quite insufficient, and she gave me terrible descriptions of the faces she used to see looking out, ravenous and imploring. She remembered that the bones protruded from the knuckles of one old man as he clutched the bars. She used to pile loaves of bread in her little boat, row across to the tower, and fix the loaves on the end of an oar so that she could pass them up to the window, and she would then see the mad people snatching the bread apart and devouring it. And when the cherries on the great tree were ripe she used to climb up into the branches and bend them against the window so that they might gather the fruit themselves from among the leaves, and she herself would gather all she could reach and throw them in. They had not even straw to sleep on. When one of them died, the body was taken out, and this was all the care they had. Such were the horrors in a town where people across the river quietly ate and slept, and the church-bells rang all day.

CHAPTER VII

Bon Papa

MY most vivid recollections of Grandfather de Rosval place him at Landerneau, where he would stop with us on his way to Quimper during his tours of inspection. His arrivals in the sleepy little town were great affairs and caused immense excitement: post-chaise, postilion,[29] whips cracking, horns blowing, and a retinue of Parisian servants. We children never had more than a glimpse of him at first, for he withdrew at once to his own rooms to rest and go through his papers. When he made his entry into the salon,–the salon of the slippery parquet and the nodding mandarins,–all the household was ranged on each side, as if for the arrival of a sovereign, and we had all to drop deep curtseys before him.

He was a rather imposing figure, with splendid clothes, the coat thickly embroidered along the edge with golden oak-leaves, and a fine, handsome head; but he was enormously, even ridiculously, stout. With an often terrifying and even repellent severity he mingled the most engaging playfulness, and our childish feelings toward him were strangely compounded of dislike and admiration.

---

[29] One who rides the near horse to guide the horses drawing a coach

Grandfather de Rosval

Grandfather de Rosval

When he arrived in the salon a lackey came behind him, carrying a large linen bag filled with a sweetmeat bought at Seugnot's, the great Parisian confectioner. I always associate these sweetmeats with *bon papa*. They were called *croquignoles*, were small, hard, yet of the consistency of soft chalk when one bit into them, and glazed with pink, white, or yellow. After the salutations, *bon papa* would take up his position before the mantelpiece and beckon the servant to give him the bag of *croquignoles*. We children, quivering with excitement, each of us already provided with a small basket, stood ready, and as *bon papa*, with a noble gesture, scattered the handfuls of *croquignoles* far and wide, we flung ourselves upon them, scrambling, falling, and filling our baskets, with much laughter and many recriminations. Then, besides the little case for *maman*, also from Seugnot's, filled with tablets of a delicious *sucre-de-pomme* in every flavor, were more dignified presents, bracelets and rings for her and for our *Tante de Laisieu* and boxes of beautiful toys for us. The only cloud cast over these occasions was that after having distributed all his bounties, *bon papa* sat down, drew a roll of manuscript from his pocket, and composed himself to read in a sonorous voice, poems of his own composition. Their theme, invariably, was the delight of reentering one's family and country, and they were very pompous and very long, sometimes moving *bon papa* almost to tears. The comic scene of family prayers that followed was pure relief, for even we children felt it comic to see *bon papa* praying.

"And are they good children?" he would ask. "Have they said their prayers?"

"Not yet, *mon père*," *maman* would answer. "They always say their prayers at bedtime." But *bon papa* was not to be so deterred from yet another ceremony.

"Good, good!" he would reply. "We will all say the evening prayers together, then."

And when we had all obediently knelt down around the room, *bon papa* recited the prayers in the same complacent, sonorous voice, making magnificent signs of the cross the while. On one of these occasions we were almost convulsed by poor little Ernest, whom *bon papa* had taken in his arms, and who was so much alarmed by the great gestures going on over his head that he broke at last into a prolonged wail and had to be carried hastily away.

One of *bon papa's* poetic works I can still remember, of a very different and more endearing character. I was taken ill one morning while we were living with him in Paris and had been given to console me by a cousin of ours staying with us, the Duchesse de M——, a delicious little purse in white, knitted silk, embroidered with pale blue forget-me-nots. I told *maman* that I wished very much to show this purse to *bon papa*, and that he should be informed of my illness. So I wrote him a note, and it was taken, with the purse, to his room. Presently the little parcel, much heavier, was brought back to me, and on opening my purse, I found inside it a centime, a liard, a sou — every coin, in fact, up to and including a golden twenty-franc piece. And this is the poem that was sent with the purse:

"Vous voulez jeune Princesse
Que je me rends près de vous?
Que je baise de votre altesse
Les pieds, les mains, et les genoux?
Dans un instant je vais me render
A vos désirs et à vos voeux,
Mais vous me permettrez de prendre
Deux baisers sur vos beaux yeux bleus."

Such a grandfather, it must be admitted, had advantages as well as charms, yet our memory of him was always clouded by the one or two acts of cruel severity we had witnessed and of which I could not trust myself to speak.

CHAPTER VIII

Le Marquis de Ploeuc

IN the Château de Ker-Guélegaan, near Quimper, lived an old friend of my family's, the Marquis de Ploeuc. The château was one of the oldest in Finisterre, an immense weather-beaten pile with a moat, a drawbridge, a great crenellated tower, and a turret that, springing from the first story, seemed, with its high-pointed roof, to be suspended in the air. Tall, dark trees rose in ordered majesty about the château, and before it a wide band of lawn, called a *tapis vert*,[30] ran to the lodge-gates that opened on the highroad. From the upper windows one saw the blue Brittany sea. Along the whole length of the front façade ran a stone terrace with seven wide steps; the windows of the *salle d'honneur* opened upon this, and the windows of the *petit salon* and the dining- and billiard-room. The furniture in the *salle d'honneur* was of Louis XV white lacquer, court chairs, and *tabourets*[31] *de cour*. There were tall mirrors all along the walls, and in the corners hung four great crystal chandeliers. The curtains and portières were of a heavy, white silk that had become gray with time; they were scattered with bouquets of faded flowers, and caught up and looped together with knots of ribbon that had once been rose-colored. This glacial and majestic room was seldom used; it was in the *petit salon*, heading from it, that guests usually sat. Here the chairs were carved along their tops with garlands of roses and ribbons so delicate that we children were specially forbidden to touch them. The walls were hung with tapestries, at which I used often to gaze with delight. One saw

---

[30] Green rug
[31] Stools

life-sized ladies and gentlemen dancing in stately rounds or laughing under trees and among flowers and butterflies. The great dining-room was paneled with dark wood carved into frames around the portraits of ancestors that were ranged along it. The coffers and the sideboards, where the silver stood, were of the same carved wood. I remember once going down to peep at the kitchen in the basement, and the dark immensity, streaming, as it were, with cooks, servants, kitchen-boys, and maids, so bewildered and almost frightened me that I never ventured there again.

"He was a splendid old gentleman"

"He was a splendid old gentleman"

The old marquis was a widower, and his married daughters, the Marquise de L— and Mme. d' A—, usually lived with him and his unmarried daughter Rosine, who became a nun. He was a splendid old gentleman, tall, with a noble carriage and severe, yet radiant, countenance. In the daytime he dressed always in gray coat and knee-breeches, with gray-and-black striped stockings and buckled shoes. At night his thick, white hair was gathered into a *catogan*,–a little square black-silk bag, that is to say,–tied with a bow, and he wore a black-silk suit. On festal occasions, Christmas, Easter, or his fête-day, he became a magnificent figure in brocaded coat and white-satin waistcoat and knee-breeches; he had diamond shoe- and knee-buckles, diamond buttons on his waistcoat, and golden *aiguillettes* looped across his breast and shoulder.

"The château was one of the oldest in Finisterre"

"The château was one of the oldest in Finisterre"

The diamond buckles he left to me, to be given to me on my first communion, and in his lifetime he had made for me a beautiful missal bound in white parchment and closed with a diamond and emerald clasp; inside were old illuminations.

In his youth M. de Ploeuc had been an officer of the Chouans, and he was, of course, a passionate royalist. He always wore the Croix de St. Louis, a fleur-de-lis, with the little cross attached by blue ribbon. I asked him once if it was the same sort of decoration as my Grandfather de Rosval's, which, I said, was larger and was tied with red, and I remember the kindly and ironic smile of my old friend as he answered, "Oh, no; that is only the Légion d'honneur."

Brittany had many marquises, some of them also old and distinguished; but he was the *doyen*[32] of them all, and was always called simply *le* marquis. Any disputes or difficulties among the local *noblesse* were always brought to him for his decision, and on such occasions, if the discussions became heated, he would say, "*Palsan bleu, mes seigneurs, il me semble que vous vous oubliez ici,*" using the dignified oath already becoming obsolete. His French was the old French of the court. He never, for instance, said, "*Je vous remercie,*" but, "*Je vous rends gráce.*"

---

[32] Oldest person

"Guests at Ker-Guélegaan arrived
with their own horses and carriages"

*"Guests at Ker-Guélegaan arrived with their own
horses and carriages"*

Guests at Ker-Guélegaan arrived with their own horses and
carriages to stay a month or more, and open house was kept.
Breakfast was at six for those who did not take communion at
the mass that was celebrated every morning in the chapel
adjoining the château; these breakfasted on returning. It was
permissible for ladies, at this early hour, to appear very
informally in *peignoirs* and *bigoudics*. *Bigoudics* are curl-papers or
ribbons. The marquis almost always took communion, but he
usually appeared at the six o'clock breakfast. After mass, once his
correspondence dealt with, he played billiards with Rosine, the

beautiful girl who became a nun in the order of the Carmelites, an order so strict that those who entered it died, to all intents and purposes, since their relatives never saw them again, and at that time were not even informed of their death. I see Rosine very clearly, bending over the billiard-table under her father's fond gaze, and I can also see her kneeling to pray in a corner of the *petit salon*. It was with such simplicity that any suspicion of affectation or parade was out of the question. In the midst of a conversation she would gently ask to be excused and would go there apart and pray, sometimes for an hour. The ladies quietly gossiping over their embroidery-frames took it quite as a matter of course that Rosine should be praying near them.

Déjeuner was at ten, and it was then that one saw how strongly feudal customs still survived at Ker-Guélegaan. The marquis sat at the head of the table, and behind his chair stood his old servant Yvon, dressed in Breton mourning-costume in memory of his defunct mistress; that is to say, in blue, black, and yellow. The other servants wore the livery of the house. Half-way down the table the white cloth ended, and the lower half had a matting covering. Here sat all the farmers of Ker-Guélegaan and their families, taking their midday meal with their master, while M. de Ploeuc and his guests and family sat above. We children were usually placed at a little side-table. The meal always began by M. de Ploeuc rising and blessing the company with two outstretched fingers, like a bishop, and he then recited a benediction. He was always served first, another survival of patriarchal custom, forced upon him, rather, for I remember his protesting against it and wishing my mother, who sat next him, to be served before him; but she would not hear of it. During the repasts a violinist and a *biniou* -player, dressed in his Breton costume, played to us.

After luncheon the ladies drove or rode or walked as the fancy took them, or, assembled in the *petit salon*, talked over their work. On hot days the blinds would be drawn down before the open windows, but in the angle of each window was fixed a long slip of mirror, so that from every corner one could see if visitors, welcome or unwelcome, were driving up to the *perron*.[33] *Goûter*, at

---

[33] Flight of steps

three, consisted of bread, fruit, and milk, and dinner was at five. After that the ladies and gentlemen assembled in the *petit salon* and talked, told ghost-stories and legends, or played games till the very early bedtime of the place and period.

This was the *train de vie* at Ker-Guélegaan; but my memories of the place center almost entirely around the figure of my old friend. I was his constant companion. When he rode out after luncheon to visit his farms, I would sit before him on his old horse Pluton. He never let Pluton gallop for fear of tiring him. "Do you see, *ma petite*," he would say, "Pluton is a comrade who has never failed me. He has earned a peaceful old age." We passed, in the wood behind the château, a monument of a Templar that frightened and interested me. He lay with his hands crossed over his sword, his feet stayed against a couchant hound, and I could not understand why he wore a knitted coat. My old friend burst out laughing when I questioned him, and said that I was as ignorant as a little carp, and that it was high time I went to the Sacré Coeur. He told me that the knitted coat was a coat of mail, and tried to instill a little history into my mind, telling me of the crusades and St. Louis; but I am afraid that my mind soon wandered away to Pluton's gently pricked ears and to the wonders of the woods that surrounded us. We had walks together, too, and went one day to the sea-shore, where there was a famous grotto often visited by strangers. When we arrived at the black arch among the rocks and I heard it was called the Devil's Grot, I was terrified, clinging to M. de Ploeuc's hand and refusing to enter.

"But why not, Sophie? Why not?" he questioned me. "I am here to take care of you, and there is no danger at all. See, Yann is lighting the torches to show us the way."

"But the devil – the devil will get me," I whispered; "Jeannie told me so."

Jeannie, indeed, was in the habit of punishing or frightening me by tales of the devil and his fork and tail and flames, and of how he would come and carry off disobedient little girls; so it was not to be wondered at that I feared to enter his grot. I imagined that he himself lurked there and would certainly carry me off, for I was well aware that I was often very disobedient. M. de Ploeuc sat down on a rock, took me on his knee, and said:

"It is very wrong of Jeannie to fill your head with such nonsense, my little one. Nothing like her devil exists in the whole world, and you must pay no attention to her stories."

He told me that the cavern was filled with beautiful stalactites, like great clusters of diamonds, and was so gentle and merry and reasonable that the devil was exorcised from my imagination forever, and I consented to enter the grotto.

Yann and the guide, a young farmer of Ker-Guélegaan, led us in with the lighted torches, and I suddenly saw before me, strangely illuminated, a somber, yet gorgeous, fairy-land. Diamonds indeed! Pillars of diamonds rose from the rocky floor to the roof, and pendants hung in long clusters, glittering in inconceivable vistas of splendor. I was so dazzled and amazed that I gave the vaguest attention to M. de Ploeuc's explanation of the way in which the stalactites were formed among the rocks. Indeed, that night I could not sleep, still seeing diamond columns and pillars, and my dear old friend was full of self-reproach next day when he heard that during the night the Devil's Grot had given me a fever.

Sometimes the Marquis de L— accompanied us on our expeditions, and sometimes I was even left in his charge for an afternoon. I disliked this very much, for he had no amusing stories to tell me and walked very fast, and when my pace flagged, he would pause to look at me reproachfully, tapping his foot on the ground, and crying, "Get up! Get up!"

M. de Ploeuc often took me, after lunch, into his little study and played the flute to me. I liked being in the study, but it rather frightened me to see my old friend remove his teeth before beginning to play. Their absence sadly altered his beautiful and stately countenance, and gave, besides, an odd, whistling timbre to his music. Still, I listened attentively, looking away now and then from his rapt, concentrated countenance to the *tapis vert* outside, where the cows were cropping the short grass, or glancing around rather shrinkingly at the headless bust of Marie Antoinette that stood on the mantelpiece. The head lay beside the bust, and there was, even to my childish imagination, a terrible beauty in the proud shoulders thus devastated. This was one of two such busts that had been decapitated by the Revolutionists. The other belonged, I think, later on, to the Empress Eugénie. When the marquis had finished his thin, melancholy airs, it was my turn to perform, and that I liked much better. I saw that he loved to hear the old Breton songs sung in my sweet, piping little voice, and it was especially pleasant, our music over, to be rewarded by being given chocolate pastils from a little enamel box that stood on the writing-desk. While I softly crunched the pastils, M. de Ploeuc told me about the countries where the plant from which the chocolate came grew. It was not at all common in Brittany at that time, and the pastils much less sweet than our modern bon bons. M. de Ploeuc also carried for his own delectation small violet and peppermint lozenges in a little gold box that he drew from his waistcoat-pocket, and these gave the pleasantest fragrance to his kiss. I often sat on with him in the study, looking at the pictures in the books he gave me while he read or wrote. He wore on the third finger of his right hand an odd black ring that had a tiny magnifying-glass fixed upon it, and while he read his hand moved gently across the page.

I owe a great deal to this dear old friend. He took the deepest interest in my deportment, and *maman* was especially delighted that he should extirpate from my speech provincial words and intonations. He entirely broke me of the bad habits of shrugging my shoulders and biting my nails.

"Only wicked men and women bite their nails," he told me, and pointed out to me as a terrible warning the beautiful and coquettish Mme. de G—, one of his guests, who had bitten her nails to the quick and quite ruined the appearance of her hands.

"And is she so wicked?" I asked. At which he laughed a little, and said that she must become so if she continued to bite her nails. He made me practice coming into and going out of a room until he was satisfied with my ease and grace.

"Do you see, *ma petite Sophie*," he said, "a woman, when she walks well, is a goddess. Walk always as if on clouds, lightly and loftily. Or imagine that you are skimming over fields of wheat, and that not an ear must bend beneath your tread."

"Maman wrote secretly to bon papa in Paris"

CHAPTER IX

Loch-Ar-Brugg

AND now I must tell of Loch-ar-Brugg, the center of my long life and the spot dearest to me upon earth. It was situated amidst the beautiful, wild, heathery country that stretched inland from Landerneau. I first saw it one day when I drove over from Landerneau with my father, and my chief recollection of this earliest visit is the deep shade under the high arch of the beech avenue and the aromatic smell of black currants in an upper room where we were taken to see the liqueur in process of being made. I was given some to drink in a tiny glass, and I never smell or taste *cassis* that the scent, color, warmth, and sweetness of that long-distant day does not flash upon me. The liqueur was being made by the farmer's wife; for part of the house, which, as I have said, papa at that time used only as a hunting-lodge, was inhabited by a Belgian farmer and his family. They were all seated at their midday meal when we arrived, and another thing I remember is that the eldest daughter, a singularly beautiful creature, with sea-green eyes and golden hair, was so much confused at seeing us that she put a spoonful of the custard she was eating against her cheek instead of into her mouth, greatly to my delight and to papa's.

"Monsieur must excuse her," said the mother; "she is very timid." On which my father replied with some compliment which made all the family smile. I see them all smiling and happy, yet it must have been soon after that a tragedy befell them. News was brought to my father that the farmer had hanged himself. The poor man's rent was badly in arrears, but when he had last spoken to my father about it, the latter, as was always his wont in such circumstances, told him not to torment himself and that he could pay when he liked. *Maman* always suspected that my father's agent had threatened the poor fellow and that he had done away with himself in an access of despondency. Papa, overcome with grief, hastened to Loch-ar-Brugg and remained there for a week with the mourning family. He gave them money to return to Belgium, and the beautiful young daughter became, we heard, a very skilful lace-maker.

"As a country gentleman he had
lived and as a country gentleman he intended to go on living"

*"As a country gentleman he had lived
and as a country gentleman he intended to go on living"*

I was too young for this lugubrious event to cast a shadow on my dear Loch-ar-Brugg, but for many years *maman* disliked the place. We still lived at Quimper or Landerneau, using Loch-ar-Brugg as a mere country resort; but by degrees the ugly walls, nine feet high, that shut in the house from the gardens and shut out the view were pulled down, lawns were thrown into one another, great clumps of blue hydrangeas were planted all down the avenue, on each side, between each beech-tree, and the house, if not beautiful, was made comfortable and convenient. It was when we were really established at Loch-ar-Brugg that *maman* began to take the finances of the household into her capable hands. She reproached my father with his lack of ambition, and asked him frequently why he did not find an occupation, to which he always replied, "*Ma chère,* I have precisely the occupations I care for." *Maman* wrote secretly to *bon papa* in Paris and begged him to find a post for her husband there, and an excellent one was found at the treasury. But when the letter came, and *maman,* full of joy, displayed it to him, papa cheerfully, but firmly, refused to consider for a moment any such change in his way of life. As a country gentleman he had lived and as a country gentleman he intended to go on living, and so indeed he continued to the end of his long life. I don't imagine that he made any difficulties as to *maman* taking over the financial management. He was quite incapable of saying no to a farmer who asked to have his rent run on unpaid, and realized, no doubt, that his methods would soon bring his family to ruin. So it was *maman* who received and paid out all the money. I see her now, sitting at the end of the long table in the kitchen, between two tall tallow candles, the peasants kneeling on the floor about her while she assessed their indebtedness and received their payments. She was never unkind, but always strict, and I was more than once the sympathetic witness of an incident that would greatly have incensed her. My father, meeting a disconsolate peasant going to an interview with *la Maîtresse,* would surreptitiously slide the needful sum into his hand! What would *maman* have said had she known that the money so brightly and briskly paid to her had just come out of her husband's pocket!

"My father, meeting a disconsolate
peasant, . . . would surreptitiously
slide the needful sum into his hand"

*"My father, meeting a disconsolate peasant...
would surreptitiously slide the needful sum into his hand"*

I was always a great deal with papa at Loch-ar-Brugg. At first
I used to walk with him, – when he did not take me on his horse,
– trotting along beside him, my hand in his. Later on, when
Tante Rose had given me a dear little pony, I rode with him, and
he had secretly made for me, knowing that *maman* would not
approve, a very astonishing riding-costume. It had long, tightly
fitting trousers, a short little jacket, like an Eton jacket, with a
red-velvet collar,–red was my father's racing color,–and on my
long golden curls a high silk hat. *Maman* burst out laughing when
she saw me thus attired and was too much amused to be

displeased. She herself rode a great deal at this time, but it was to hunting- and shooting-parties, from which she would return with her "bag" hanging from a sort of little pole fixed to her saddle; and I remember that one day she brought a strange beast that none of us ever saw in Brittany again, a species of armadillo (*tatou*) that her horse had trodden upon and killed.

It was at Loch-ar-Brugg, on one of these early walks with papa, that my first vivid recollection of a landscape seen as a beautiful picture comes to me. We had entered a deep lane where gnarled old trees interlaced their fingers overhead and looked, with their twisted trunks, like crouching men or beasts; and as we advanced, it became so dark and mysterious that I was very much frightened and hung to papa's hand, begging to be taken out. He pointed then before us, and far, far away I saw a tiny spot of light. "Don't be frightened, Sophie," he said; "we are going toward the sunlight." So I kept my eyes fixed on the widening spot, holding papa's hand very tightly in the haunted darkness; and when we suddenly emerged, we were on the brink of a great gorge, and beyond were mountains, and below us lay a tranquil, silver lake. I have never forgotten the strange, visionary impression, as of a beauty evoked from the darkness. Papa told me the story of the lake; it was called "le lac des Korrigans." The Korrigans are Breton fairies – fairies, I think, more melancholy than those of other lands, and with something sinister and *macabre* in their supernatural activities. They danced upon the turf, it is true, in fairy-rings, but also, at night, they would unwind the linen from the dead in the churchyards and wash it in this lake. I felt the same fear and wonder on hearing this story that all my descendants have shown when they, in their turn, have come to hear it, and my little granddaughter, in passing near the lake with me, has often said, shrinking against me, "Je ne veux pas voir les blanchisseuses, Grand'mère."

Le Lac des Korrigans

Le Lac des Korrigans

Unlike the marquis, who filled my mind, or tried to fill it, with the facts of nature and history, papa, on our walks, told me all these old legends, not as if he believed them, it is true, but as if they were stories quite as important in their way as the crusades; and perhaps he was right.

Sometimes, when we were walking or riding, we met convicts who had escaped from the great prison at Brest. I was strictly forbidden ever to go outside the gates alone; but once, at evening, I slipped out and ran along the road to meet papa, who, I knew, was coming from Landerneau on foot. He was very much perturbed when he saw me emerge before him in the dusk, and drew me sharply to his side, and I then noticed that two men were following him. Presently they joined us and asked papa, very roughly, for the time.

"It is nine, I think," said my father, eyeing them very attentively.

"You think? Haven't you a watch, then?" said one of them.

I suppose they imagined that the rifle papa carried over his shoulder was unloaded; but unslinging it in the twinkling of an eye, he said sternly:

"Walk ahead. If you turn or stop, I shoot." They obeyed at once, and as they went along we heard a queer clink come from their ankles.

"Escaped convicts," said papa in a low voice. "Poor devils! And you see, Sophie, how dangerous it is for little girls to wander on the road at night."

"Papa took out his hunting-flask and made him drink"

"Papa took out his hunting-flask and made him drink"

On another occasion we found a wretched, exhausted man lying by the roadside, and papa stopped and asked him what the matter was. He must have felt the kindness of the face and voice, for he said:

"I am an escaped convict, monsieur. For God's sake! don't betray me. I am dying of hunger." Papa took out his hunting-flask and made him drink, and then, when we saw that the brandy had given him strength, he put some money into his hand and said:

"It is against the law that I should help you, but I give you an hour before I raise the alarm. Go in that direction, and God be with you!"

The church-bells were rung everywhere, answering one another from village to village when a convict was known to be at large; but on this occasion I know that my father did not fulfill his duty, the poor creature's piteous face had too much touched him. Once, too, when we children were walking with Jeannie along the highroad we caught sight of a beggar-woman sleeping in the ditch. In peering over cautiously to have a good look at her, we saw huge men's boots protruding from beneath her petticoats, and, at the other end, a black beard, and we then made off as fast as our legs would carry us, realizing that the beggar-woman was a convict in disguise. At an inn not far from Loch-ar-Brugg there was a woman of bad character who sold these disguises to the escaped convicts.

"A woman of bad character, who sold
these disguises to escaped convicts"

*"A woman of bad character, who sold
these disguises to escaped convicts"*

Papa and my little brother and sister (Maraquita was not then
born) were not my only companions at Loch-ar-Brugg. The
property of Ker-Azel adjoined ours, and I saw all my Laisieu
cousins continually, dear, gentle France, domineering Jules, and
the rest. There were nine of them. It was Jules who told us one
day that he had been thinking over the future of France (the
country, not his brother), and had come to the conclusion that
we should all soon suffer from a terrible famine. Famines had
come before this, said Jules, so why not again? It was only wise
to be prepared for them; and what he suggested was that we
should all accustom ourselves to eat grass and clover, as the

cattle did. If it nourished cows, it would nourish us. All that was needed was a little good-will in order that we should become accustomed to the new diet. Jules was sincerely convinced of the truth of what he said; but he was a tyrannous boy, and threatened us with beatings if we breathed a word of his plan to our parents. We were to feign at meals that we were not hungry, and to say that we had eaten before coming to the table. I well remember the first time that we poor little creatures knelt down on all fours in a secluded meadow and began to bite and munch the grass. We complained at once that we did not like it at all, and Jules, as a concession to our weakness, said that we might begin with clover, since it was sweeter. For some time we submitted to the ordeal, getting thinner and thinner and paler, growing accustomed, it is true, to our tasteless diet and never daring to confess our predicament; we were really afraid of the famine as well as of Jules. At last our parents, seriously alarmed, consulted the good old doctor, as nothing could be got from us but stout denials of hunger. He took me home with him, for I was his special pet, and talked gravely and gently to me, reminding me that I was now eight years old and of the age of reason, going to confession and capable of sin. It was a sin to tell lies, and if I would tell him the truth, he would never betray my confidence. Thus adjured, I began to cry, and confessed that we had all been eating nothing but grass and clover. The doctor petted and consoled me, told me that it was all folly on the part of Jules, and that he would set it right without anyone knowing that I had told him. He kept his promise to me. It was as if by chance he found us all in our meadow next day, on all fours, munching away. Jules sprang up, sulky and obstinate.

"Yes, we are eating grass and clover," he said, "and we are quite accustomed to it now and like it very much, and we shall be better off than the rest of you when the famine comes."

The doctor burst out laughing, and his laughter broke the spell Jules had cast upon us. He told us that not only was there no probability of a famine, no possibility even, France being a country rich in food, but that even were there to be a famine, we should certainly all be dead before it came if we went on eating as the cattle did, since we were not accommodated with the same digestive apparatus as they. He described to us this apparatus and our own, and at last even Jules, who was as thin and as weary as the rest of us, was convinced, and glad to be convinced. It was not till many years afterward that we told our parents the story.

One day we children were all in a deep lane—perhaps the same that had frightened me years before—when, at a turning, the most inconceivable monster towered above us in the gloom. We recognized it in a moment as a camel (a camel in Brittany!), and with it came a band of Gipsies, with dark skins, flashing teeth, bright handkerchiefs, and ear-rings. Our alarm was not diminished when we saw that they led, as well as the camel, two thin performing bears. But as we emerged into the light with the chattering, fawning crowd, alarm gave way to joyous excitement. The camel and the bears were under perfect control, and the Gipsies were not going to hurt us. They asked if they might make the bears dance for us, and we ran to show them the way to Loch-ar-Brugg. *Maman*, in her broad garden hat, was walking in the beech-avenue, and came at once to forbid the Gipsies to enter, as they were preparing to do; but as we supplicated that we should be allowed to see the bears dance, she consented to allow the performance to take place in the high-road before the *grille*. We sat about on the grass; the camel towered against the sky, gaunt, tawny, and melancholy; and the bears, armed with wooden staffs, went through their clumsy, reluctant tricks. *Maman*, from within the *grille*, surveyed the entertainment with great disfavor, and it lost its charm for us when we heard her say: "How wretchedly thin and miserable the poor creatures look! They must be dying of hunger." We then became very sorry for the bears, too, and glad to have them left in peace, and while we distributed sous[34] to the Gipsies, *maman* went to the house and returned with a basket of broken bread and meat, which she gave to the famished beasts. How they snatched and devoured it, and how plainly I see *maman* standing there, the deep green vault of the avenue behind her, the clumps of blue hydrangeas, her light dress, her wide-brimmed garden hat, and her severe,

---

[34] Coins

87

solicitous blue eyes as she held out the bread to the hungry bears!

"A great character at Loch-ar-Brugg was the curé"

"A great character at Loch-ar-Brugg was the curé"

A great character at Loch-ar-Brugg was the curé. It was he who had baptized me, for I was baptized not at Quimper, but in the little church of St. Eloi that stood at the foot of the Loch-ar-Brugg woods and had been in the Kerouguet family for generations. During my earliest years there he was our chaplain, inhabiting one of the *pavillons*[35] in the garden with his old servant; later on he was given the living of Plougastel, some miles away, and my father had to persuade him to accept it, for he was very

---

[35] Detached house

averse to leaving Loch-ar-Brugg and our family. Still, even at Plougastel we saw him constantly; he drove over nearly every day in his little pony-trap, and officiated every Sunday at the seven o'clock mass at St. Eloi. What a dear, honest fellow he was, and what startling sermons I have heard him preach! Once he informed his congregation that they would all be damned like Jean-Jacques Rousseau and Fénélon! This threat, pronounced in Breton, was especially impressive, and how he came by the two ill-assorted names I cannot imagine, for he was nearly as ignorant of books as his flock. He was devoted to my father body and soul, being the son of one of his farmers. They were great comrades. Whenever my father had had a good day's shooting he would go to the *pavillon* and cry: "Come to dinner! There are woodcocks." And the curé never failed to come. I see him now, with his rustic, rugged face, weather-tanned, gay, and austere. One of my first memories is of the small, square neck ornament (*rabat*) that the clergy wear,–a *bavette*[36] we children called them,–stitched round with white beads. I longed for these beads, and when he took me on his knee I always fixed my eyes upon them. Unattainable indeed they seemed, but one day, noticing the intentness of my gaze, he questioned me, and I was able to express my longing. "But you shall have the beads!" he cried, touched and delighted. "I have two *rabats*, and one is old and past wearing. Nothing is simpler than to cut off the beads for you, my little Sophie."

His performance was even better than his promise, for he brought me a bagful of the beads, collected from among his curé friends, and for days I was blissfully occupied in making chains, rings, and necklaces. Some of these ornaments survived for many years.

---

[36] Bib

"Je me sauve," he would exclaim

"Je me sauve," he would exclaim

The curé was not at all happy in the presence of fine people. *"Je me sauve!"* he would exclaim if such appeared, and he would make off to the garden, where he was altogether at home, true son of the soil that he was. Here he would gird up his *soutane*[37] over his homespun knee-breeches, open his coarse peasant's shirt on his bare chest, and prune and dig and plant; and when he took a task in hand it went quickly. One of my delights was when he put me into the wheelbarrow and trundled me off to Ker-Eliane to dig up ferns for *maman's* garden.

He, too, told me many legends. The one of St. Eloi especially interested me. St. Eloi was the son of a blacksmith and helped

---

[37] Cassock

his father at the forge in the tiny hamlet called after him. One day as they were working, a little child came riding up, mounted on a horse so gigantic that four men could not have held him. "Will you shoe my horse, good friends?" said the child, – who of course was *l'Enfant Jésus*, – very politely. "His shoe is loose, and his hoof will be hurt." The father blacksmith looked with astonishment and indignation at the horse, and said that he could not think of shoeing an animal of such a size; but the son, St. Eloi, said at once that he would do his best. So *l'Enfant Jésus* slid down, and took a seat on the *talus* in front of the smithy, and St. Eloi at once neatly unscrewed the four legs of the horse and laid them down beside the enormous body. At this point in the story I always cried out:

"But, *Monsieur le Curé*, did it not hurt the poor horse to have its legs unscrewed?"

And the curé, smiling calmly, would reply:

"Not in the least. You see, this was a miracle, my little Sophie."

So St. Eloi was able to deal with the great hoofs separately, and when all was neatly done, the legs were screwed on again; and the child remounted, and said to St. Eloi's father before he rode away:

"You are a little soured with age, my friend. Your son here is very wise. Listen to him and take his advice in everything, for it will be good."

It was no doubt on account of this legend that all the horses through all the country far and near were brought to the church of St. Eloi once a year to be blessed by the curé. This ceremony was called *le Baptême des Chevaux*. The horses, from plow-horses to carriage-horses and hunters, were brought and ranged round the church in groups of fours and sixes. At the widely opened western door, the curé stood, holding the *goupillon*, or holy-water sprinkler, and the horses were slowly led round the church, row after row, seven times, and each time that they passed before him the curé sprinkled them with holy water. After this initial blessing the curé took up his stand within beside the christening-font, and the horses were led into the church,–I so well remember the dull thud and trampling of their feet upon the earthen floor,–and the curé, with holy water from the font, made the sign of the cross upon each large, innocent forehead. Finally the tail of each horse was carefully cut off, and all the tails hung up in the church together, to be sold for the benefit of the church at the end of the year, before *le Baptême des Chevaux* took place again. This touching ceremony still survives, but the horses are only led round the church and blessed, not brought inside.

The Church of St. Eloi was very ancient, and adorned with strange old statues of clumsily carved stone painted in garish colors. One was of a Christ waiting for the cross, His hands tied before Him. It was a hideous figure, the feet and hands huge and distorted, the eyes staring like those of a doll; yet it had an impressive look of suffering. There were no benches in the church except for our family, near the choir. The peasants, the men on one side, the women on the other, knelt on the bare earth during the office. They had used, always, when they entered the church, to pass round before *les maîtres*, bowing before them; but even my mother objected to this, and the curé was told to give out from the pulpit that *les maîtres* were no longer to be bowed to in church, where there was only one master. *Maman*, however, did not at all like it that my father should insist on us children kneeling with the peasants, and it was the one subject on which I remember a difference of opinion between my grandfather Rosval and papa. But the latter was firm, and Ernest on the side of the men, Eliane and I on the side of the women, we knelt through mass. This was no hardship to us, for the kind peasants spread their skirts for our little knees and regaled us all through the service with *crêpes*.

Crêpes seem to be present in nearly all my Breton memories. The peasants made them for us when we went to visit them in their cottages, and it would have hurt their feelings deeply had we refused them. We children delighted in these visits not only on account of the *crêpes*, but on account of the picturesque interest of these peasant interiors. The one living-room had an earthen floor and a huge chimney-place of stone, often quaintly carved, and so large that chairs could be set within it about the blazing logs. The room was paneled, as it were, with beds that looked, when their sliding wooden doors were closed, like tall wardrobes ranged along the walls. They were usually of dark old wood and often beautifully carved. A narrow space between the tops of these beds and the ceiling allowed some air (but what air!) to reach the sleepers, and, within, the straw was piled high, and the mattress and feather bed were laid upon it. It was quite customary for father, mother, and three or four children to sleep in one bed, several generations often occupying a room, as well as the servants, who were of the same class as their masters. The beds were climbed into by means of a carved chest that stood beside them. These were called *huches*, and contained the heirloom costumes, a store of bread, and the Sunday shoes! Potatoes were kept under the bed. In the window stood the table where the family and servants all ate together, and above it hung, suspended by a pulley and string from the ceiling, a curious contrivance for holding spoons. It was a sort of wooden disk, and the spoons were held in notches cut round the edge; it was lowered when needed, and each person took a spoon. A great earthenware bowl of creamy milk stood in the center of the table, and with each mouthful of porridge, or *fare*, the spoons were dipped, in community, into the milk. *Fare* was a sort of thick porridge made of maize, allowed to cool in a large round cake, and cut in slices when cold. It was one of the peasants' staple dishes, and another was the porridge made of oatmeal, rye, or buckwheat, served hot, with a lump of butter. For breakfast they all drank *café au lait*, strange coffee boiled with the milk; fortunately milk and butter were plentiful. Of the hygienic habits of the peasants at this time the less said the better; a very minor detail was that the long hair of the men and the closely coiffed tresses of the women swarmed with vermin, and after every visit we paid, our heads were always carefully examined. One peasant, I remember, a good fellow, Paul Simur by name, of whom my father was especially fond, was so dirty and unwashed that a sort of mask of dirt had formed upon his features. One day, at a hunting-party, papa called to Paul to come and sit beside him, and the other huntsmen, with singular bad taste, began to make fun of poor Paul, who sat much abashed, with hanging head. Papa affectionately laid an arm about his neck and defended him, until his friends finally cried out that they wagered he would not kiss him. At this, although he confessed afterward to the most intense repugnance, he at once kissed Paul heartily. Poor Paul was quite overcome. He came to my father afterward with tears in his eyes and said, standing before him and gazing at him:

"*Oh, mon maître, que je t'aime!*"

"And why don't you ever wash your face, Paul?" papa asked him then, and Paul explained that he had never been taught to wash and was afraid it would seriously hurt him to begin. Papa undertook to teach him. He got soap and soda and hot water and lathered Paul, gently and firmly, until at last his very agreeable features were disinterred. Paul was perfectly delighted, and his face shone with cleanliness ever after.

Paul

Paul

A special friend of mine among the peasants was dear old Keransiflan, the lodge-keeper. I was fond of joining him while he tended the road in front of the lodge-gates and sitting on his wheelbarrow with him to talk to him while he ate his midday meal. This consisted of a huge slice of black bread thickly spread with butter, and it seemed to me that no bread and butter had ever looked so good.

One day he must have seen how much I longed for it, for he said, holding out the slice, "*Demoiselle, en veux-tu?*" I did not need to be asked twice, and can still see the great semicircle that I bit into the slice, and I was happily munching when *maman* appeared at the lodge-gates. She was very much displeased, and mainly that I should be devouring poor Keransiflan's luncheon, and she rated me so soundly that the kind old man interceded for me, saying, "*Notre maîtresse, c'est moi qui lui l'ai donné.*" I think that *maman* must have seen that it gave him great pleasure to share his bread with me; at all events, Keransiflan and I, sitting on our wheelbarrow, were allowed to go on eating in peace.

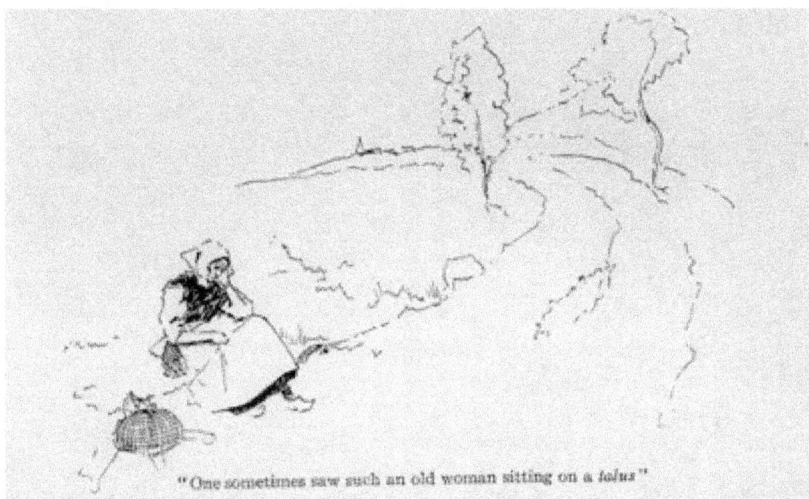

"One sometimes saw such an old woman sitting on a talus"

"One sometimes saw such an old woman sitting on a talus"

But the peasants were a hard, harsh race and pitiless in their dealings toward one another. Their treatment of their old people was terrible. If an old mother, past work, had no money, she was ruthlessly turned out to beg. One sometimes saw such an old woman sitting on a *talus*, her pitiful bundle of rags beside her, helpless and stupefied. I remember a story that was told me by one of my servants about such an old woman that she had known. She had four hundred francs, and was cared for in the family of one son until it was spent, when she was turned out. Another son more kindly took her in; but his wife was a hard woman, and though she finally consented to accept the useless old mother into the household, she grudged every sou spent upon her. Thus, though the only two joys remaining her in life were snuff and coffee, only two sous a week was allowed her for tobacco, and as for coffee, she was given never a drop. When she was dying she told the servant from whom I had the story that what made her suffer most had been to sit by in the morning and smell the delicious odor of the coffee as the others drank it. This has always seemed to me a heart-piercing story. All the Breton women smoked, by the way, and pipes, and in a curious fashion; for the bowl was turned downward, though why, I do not know.

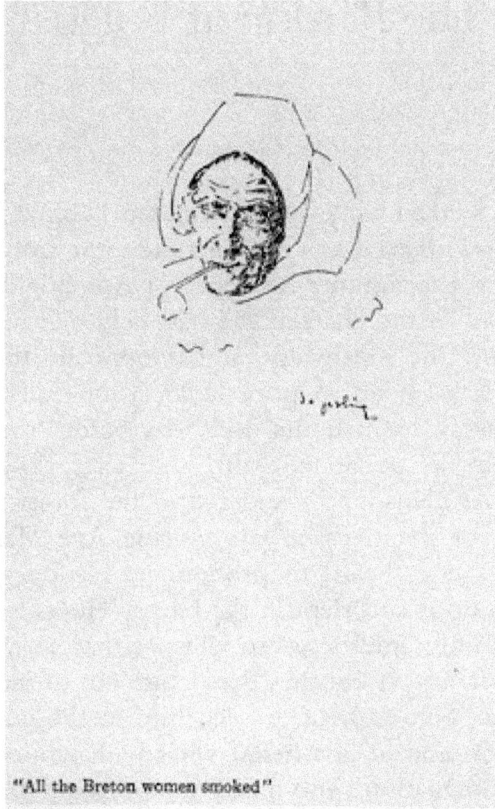

"All the Breton women smoked"

"All the Breton women smoked"

CHAPTER X

The Pardon at Folgoat

I WAS taken while I was a child at Loch-ar-Brugg to the famous *Pardon de Folgoat*, to which people came from all Brittany. In Folgoat was the summer residence of Anne de Bretagne, and in the vast hall of the château she had held her audiences. The château is now the presbytery, and is opposite the church, of which there is a legend. A poor child, Yann Salacin, who was devoid of reason, spent hours every day before the altar of the Virgin, which he decorated with the wild flowers that he gathered in the fields, and wandered in the forest, swinging on the branches of the trees, always singing Ave Maria, the only words he was ever heard to pronounce. He begged for food from door to door and slept in the barns. The peasants became impatient with him and began to whisper that he was possessed of an evil spirit, and at last they drove him out of the village. The curé, who was a good man, missed him in the church, sought vainly for him, and at last heard what had happened. He was filled with indignation, and told the peasants that they had committed a crime. Then he set out to look for poor Yann, and found him at last in a distant forest, dead with hunger. He brought the body back to Folgoat and buried it near the church, and one day he saw that a tall white lily had grown up from the grave; when he opened the grave he found that the lily sprang from the lips of the little innocent, and on the petals of the flower one could read in letters of gold Ave Maria. This legend is believed in all Brittany, and a stained-glass window in the church tells the story.

Behind the church is the Well of Love, so called because not a day passes that lovers do not come to test their fate by trying to float pins upon the surface of the water. If the pins float, all promises well, and they go away happy. Astute ones slightly grease the pins, and thus aid destiny.

But to return to the *pardon*. I remember that on this occasion an old cook in the family had permission to start two or three days before the *pardon*, so that she might go all the way on her knees, and during those days one met many such devout pilgrims making their way on their knees along the dusty roads. Some of them came from far distances. We children were called before dawn on the August morning, and it was a sleepy, half-bewildered dressing by candle-light. As a closed carriage made me sick, I was put into the coupé with papa and *maman*. Eliane, Ernest, their nurses, and all the other servants, followed in a sort of omnibus, and behind them came all the horses, trotting gaily along the road to share in the blessings of this great day of the Assumption of the Virgin. The horses of Brittany, it will be conceded, are a specially favored race. Although I was in the coupé and had all the freshness of the early air to invigorate me, I remember of the journey from Loch-ar-Brugg to Folgoat only that I was deplorably sick and the greatest inconvenience to my parents. Fortunately, I was restored the moment I set my feet upon the ground.

We children had a splendid picnic breakfast

We children had a splendid picnic breakfast

We were to be entertained for the day at Folgoat by the curé, and to lunch with him and with the bishops at the presbytery; but we were already ravenously hungry, so, although papa and *maman* must continue to fast until after taking communion at the early service, we children had a splendid picnic breakfast in the presbytery garden, and a jellied breast of lamb is my first recollection of the day at Folgoat! Then we went out to see the great festival. Seventy-five years or more have passed since that day, and it still lives in my mind with a beauty more than splendid, a divine beauty. In the vast plain, under the vast, blue sky, six bishops, glittering with gold and precious stones, celebrated mass simultaneously at six great altars among thousands of worshipers. It was a sea of color under the August sun, and the white *coiffes* of the women were like flocks of snowy doves. There was an early mass and the high mass at eleven. When this was over, we assembled at the presbytery to lunch with the bishops. The table was laid in Anne de Bretagne's council-chamber, its stone walls covered with archaic figures, and it must have been a picturesque sight to see the bishops sitting in all their splendor against that ancient background; but what I most remember are the stories they told of Louis XI and his misdeeds, which seemed to me more interesting and more cruel than the Arabian Nights and Ali Baba and his forty thieves. In the church itself was shown a superbly carved bench where, it was said, while praying, he ordered with a nod the death of a Breton noble who had refused to do him homage. When we went into the church after lunch to see this bench, I sat down on it, and my long golden curls were caught in the claws of the interlaced monsters on the back, and I hurt myself so much in wrenching myself free that I hated still more fiercely the wicked king who condemned men to death while he prayed. O the horrid monster!

Then at three came the great procession. First went the six bishops, mitered and carrying their croziers; then followed the children of the *noblesse*, we among them, all in white, with white wreaths on our heads; then all the vast multitude, twenty or thirty abreast, singing canticles, a stupendous sight and sound, all marching round the plain, from altar to altar, under the burning sun. I remember little after that. The Marquis de Ploeuc was there, his hair tied in the *catogan*, and wearing his black silk suit: I think he must have lunched with us at the curé's. It was arranged that he and his two eldest daughters were to drive back to Loch-ar-Brugg with *maman* and spend some days with us, and so, though I must have been very tired, I was to ride back beside papa on my pony, which had been duly blessed. It was already night when we started, and what a wonderful ride it was! I remember no fatigue. I still wore my white dress, and *maman* swathed my head and shoulders in a white lace shawl, and all the way back to Loch-ar-Brugg papa told me stories of hunts, of fairies, of saints, and of escaped convicts. Every group of trees, every rock, every turning in the road, had its legend or its adventure.

On the road to Loch-ar-Brugg

On the road to Loch-ar-Brugg

CHAPTER XI

Bonne Maman's Death

WE were at Quimper when *bonne maman* died. She had
been failing for some time, and her character, until then so
gentle, had altered. Mere trifles disquieted her, and she became
fretful, alarmed, and even impatient. She seemed so little in her
big bed, and, when I wanted to climb up beside her, after my
wont, she signed to Jeannie to take me away and said that it tired
her too much to see children and that the air of a sick-room was
not good for them. "Tell my daughter—tell her. They must not
come!" she repeated several times in a strange, shrill voice. I slid
down from the bed, I remember, abashed and disconcerted, and
while I longed to see my dear *bonne maman* as I had known her, I
was afraid of this changed *bonne maman*; and it hurt me more for
her than for myself that she should be so changed.

But one day when *maman* was in the room, she caught sight
of me hanging about furtively in the passage, and called out
gently to me to go away, that *bonne maman* was tired and was
going to sleep. Then a poor little voice, no longer shrill, very
trembling, came from the bed, saying: "Let her come, Eliane. It
will not hurt me. I want to see her for a moment."

I approached the bed, walking on tiptoe; the curtains were
drawn to shade *bonne maman* from the sunlight, and I softly came
and stood within them. O my poor *bonne maman!* I could hardly
recognize her. She seemed old—old and shrunken, and her eyes
no longer smiled. She looked at me so fixedly that I was
frightened, and she said to *maman:*

"Lift her up on the bed. I want to kiss her." She took my
hand then, and looked at my little finger as she always used to
do, and said: "I see that you have been very good with your

103

mother, but that you don't obey your nurse. You must always be obedient. You understand me, don't you, Sophie? Do you say your prayers?"

"Yes, *bonne maman*," I answered.

"Have you said them this morning?"

"No, *bonne maman*."

"Say them now."

I made the sign of the cross and said the following prayer, which I repeated morning and evening every day, and with slightly altered nomenclature, my children and grandchildren have repeated, as I did, until the age of reason: "*Mon Dieu*, bless me and bless and preserve *grand-père, bonne maman, maman, papa*, my sisters, my brother, Tiny" [this was my little dog], "Ghislaine, France, Kerandraon, all my family, and make me very good. Amen." When I had finished, *bonne maman* drew me gently to her, pressed me in her arms, and kissed me on my eyes.

After this, for how many days I do not remember, everything became very still in the house. The servants whispered when they had to speak, and the older people, when they met us, told us gently to go into the garden and to be very quiet. We did not see *maman* or *papa* at all. My *tante* de Laisieu was with us, and dear France. *Bon papa* arrived from Paris. One morning was very sunny and beautiful, and as I played with Eliane in the garden I forgot the oppression that weighed upon us and began to sing to her a Breton song which Jeannie had taught me. These were the words:

> Le Roy vient demain au château,
> "Ecoute moi bien, ma Fleurette,
> Tu regarderas bien son aigrette!"
>
> "Je regarderai," dit Fleurette,
> "Pour bien reconnaître le Roy!
> Mes yeux ne verront que toi,
> Et mon coeur n'aimera que toi."

While I sang I looked up at *bonne maman's* window, for I knew how fond she was of hearing me. The window was shut, and this was unusual; so I sang the louder, that she should hear me, of *Fleurette* and *le Roy*. Then France and one of the servants came running out of the house, and I saw that both had been crying, and France put his arm about me while the servant said, "Mademoiselle must not sing." And France whispered: "You will wake *bonne maman*. Go into the orchard, dear Sophie. There you will not be heard." In the evening papa came for us in the nursery, and I saw that he, too, had been crying. I had never before seen tears in his dear eyes. He took us up to *maman's* room. All the blinds were drawn down, but I could see her lying on her bed, in her white woolen *peignoir*, her arms crossed behind her head, her black jet rosary lying along the sheet beside her. We kissed her, one after the other, and I saw the great tears rolling down her cheeks.

"*Maman* – is *bonne maman* very ill?" I whispered. I felt that something terrible had happened to us all.

"My little girl," said *maman*, "your poor *bonne maman* does not suffer any more. She is very happy now with the angels and *le bon Dieu*," but *maman* was sobbing as she spoke.

I knew death only as it had come to one of my little birds that lived in the round cage hung in the nursery-window, and I was very much frightened when papa said: "I am going to take Sophie to your mother's room, Eliane. She is old enough to understand." But I went with him obediently, holding his hand. Outside *bonne maman's* door he paused and stooped to kiss me and said: "I know how much you loved your *bonne maman*, Sophie, and I want you to say good-by to her, for you will never see her again. She loved you so much, my little darling, and you shall be the last one to kiss her." The room was all black, and in the middle stood the bed. Beside it, on a table, a little *chapelle* had been made with a great silver cross and candelabra with lighted tapers. A bunch of fresh box stood in a goblet of holy water. *Bonne maman* lay with her arms stretched out before her, the hands clasped on her black wooden crucifix with a silver Christ that had always hung upon her wall. Her hair was not dressed, but drawn up from her forehead and covered with a mantilla of white silk Spanish lace, which fell down over her shoulders on each side. I stood beside her holding papa's hand. Her profile was sharply cut against the blackness, and I had never before seen how beautiful it was. Her eyes were closed, and she smiled tranquilly. I felt no longer any fear; but when papa lifted me in his arms so that I might kiss *bonne maman* and my lips touched her forehead, a great shock went through me. How cold her forehead was! O my poor *bonne maman!* Even now, after all the lusters that have passed over me, I feel the cold of that last kiss.

CHAPTER XII

The Journey *from* Brittany

IT was not long after *bonne maman's* death that we left Brittany and went to Paris to live with *bon papa*. I remember every detail of this my first long journey. The day began with a very early breakfast, which we all had together in the dining-room and at which we had the great treat of drinking chocolate. Then came the complicated business of stowing us all away in our capacious traveling-carriage. It was divided into three compartments. First came what was called the *coupé*, with windows at the sides and a large window in front from which we looked out past the coachman's red-stockinged legs and along the horses' backs to where the postilion jounced merrily against the sky in a red Breton costume like the coachman's, his long hair tied behind with black ribbon, a red jockey's cap on his head, and black shoulder-knots with jet *aiguillettes*.[38] After the *coupé*, and communicating with it by a tiny passage, though it had doors of its own, was another compartment for maids, nurses, and children, and behind that another and larger division for all the other servants. On the top were seats beside the coachman, and papa spent most of the day up there smoking. The luggage, carried on the top, was covered by a great leather covering, buckled down all over it, called a *bache*. The horses were post-horses, renewed at every post. It was decided that I was to go in the *coupé* with *maman*, papa, and little Maraquita, as I should get more fresh air there. I wore, I remember, a red cashmere dress made out of a dress of *maman's*. The material had been brought from India and was bordered with a design of palm-leaves.

---

38 An ornamental cord worn on the shoulder

Indeed, this red cashmere must have provided me with a succession of dresses, for I remember that when I made my entrée at the *Sacré Coeur* years afterwards, the bishop, visiting the convent, stopped, smiling, at my bench, and said, "Why, this is a little Republican, is it not?" Eliane and I both wore *capulets* on our heads. These were squares of white cloth that fell to the shoulders and that folded back from the forehead and fastened under the chin with bands of black velvet, a Spanish head-dress. Our cloaks were the full cloaks, gathered finely around the neck and shoulders, that *maman* had made for us, copied from the peasants' cloaks, of foulard for summer and wool for winter. Little Maraquita, who spent most of the three days' journey on *maman's* knees, wore, as always until she was seven or eight, white and pale blue, the Virgin's colors, as she had been *vouée au bleu et au blanc* after a terrible accident that had befallen her in infancy. She had fallen into the fire at Landerneau, and her head and forehead had been badly burned, and *maman* had thus dedicated her to the Virgin with prayers that she might not be disfigured–prayers that were more than answered, for Maraquita became exquisitely beautiful. Papa, I may add here, had many friends and connections in Spain; hence my little sister's name, and hence our *capulets*.

Eliane and Ernest traveled in the second compartment with their nurses, Eliane carrying Tiny and her huge doll, and Ernest, unfortunately for our peace of mind, a drum of mine that I had given him and upon which he beat the drumsticks hour after hour. *Maman*, in the *coupé*, cried out at intervals that it was intolerable to hear such an incessant noise and that the child must really, now, be made to stop; but papa always mildly soothed her, saying: "Let him play. It keeps him distracted; he would probably be crying otherwise." So Ernest continued to roll his drum. In the *coupé* I was fully occupied in playing at horses. Real leather reins had been fixed at each side of the front window, passing under it so that, looking out over the horses' haunches, I had the delightful illusion, as I wielded the reins, of really driving them. I do not remember that I was sick at all on the first day. The country was mountainous, and at every steep hill we all got out and walked down, and this also, probably helped to preserve me. One feature of the Brittany landscape of those days stands out clearly in my memory, the tall, sinister-looking telegraph-poles that stood, each one just visible to the last, on the heights of the country. When I say telegraph it must not be imagined that they were our modern electric installations, although so they were called. These were of a very primitive and very ingenious construction. At the top of each pole, by means of the projecting arm that gave it the look of a gallows, immense wooden letters were hung out, one after the other; these letters were worked by means of wires that passed down the poles into the little hut at its foot. Each wire at the bottom had a label with its corresponding letter, and the operator in the hut, by pulling the wire, pulled the letter into its place at the top of the pole, and was thus able laboriously to spell out the message he had to convey and to make it visible to the operator at the next post, who passed it on to the next. These clumsy telegrams could be sent, as far as I remember, only at certain hours of the day, and I think that it must have been during a wayside halt on this journey that I visited a hut with papa and had the system explained to me and saw a message being sent, for I remember the clatter and shaking as the big letters overhead were pulled into place. I do not know whether this method of communication was used all over France, but one or two of the old poles still survive in Brittany.

The postilion sounded his horn

The postilion sounded his horn

Our first stop that day was at Quimperlé. The postilion, as we approached a town or village, sounded his horn, and what excitement it caused in these quiet little places when we came driving up, and how all the people crowded round us!

The inn at Quimperlé was called the Hôtel du Trèfle Noir, and though very primitive, the thatch showing through the rafters in the roof of the immense kitchen-dining-room, it was scrupulously clean. We all sat down together at the long table, servants, coachman, postilion, and all, and the *déjeuner* served to us by the good landlady was fit to put before a king. I remember *maman* laughing and asking her why she served the salmon and, afterward, a heaping golden mound of fried potatoes, on a great plank, and the landlady saying that she had no dishes large enough. There was a turkey, too, stuffed with chestnuts and of course *crêpes* and cream. Next door to us, in a smaller room, a band of commercial travelers were also lunching, and as we finished each course it was carried in to those cheerful young fellows, whose hurrahs of joy added zest to our own appetites. That night we slept at Rennes, where I remember only that I was very tired and that a horrid man who came to make a fire in our bedrooms spat upon the floor, to our disgust and indignation. I remember, too, a very pleasant crisp cake, or roll, that *maman* gave me to eat before I went to bed.

It was on the third day that we drove at last into Paris, a fairy-land to my gazing, stupefied eyes. What struck me most were the fountains of the Place de la Concorde, the bronze mermaids holding the spouting fish, and the little sunken gardens, four of them, that at that time surrounded the obelisk. *Bon Papa* lived in the rue St. Dominique, St. Germain, and as we drove up to the door I remember that it was under blossoming acacia-trees and that the postilion blew a great blast upon his horn to announce our arrival. The house, which was, indeed, a very pleasing specimen of Louis XV architecture, looked palatial to my childish eyes. *Bon Papa* was standing, very portly, on the terrace to welcome us, and we ran into a park behind the house, with an avenue of horse-chestnuts and a high fountain. But Brittany was left far behind, and many, many years were to pass before I again saw my Loch-ar-Brugg.

Tin

www.ingramcontent.com/pod-product-compliance
Lightning Source LLC
Chambersburg PA
CBHW021204020426
42331CB00003B/192